LANGUAGE A[...]

Dorothy S. Str[...]
Celia Genishi and Don[...]
ADVISORY BOARD: *Richard Allington,*
Anne Haas Dyson, Carole Edelsky, Mary Juzwik, Susan Lytle, Django Paris, Timothy Shanahan

continued

For volumes in the NCRLL Collection (edited by JoBeth Allen and Donna E. Alvermann) and the Practitioners Bookshelf Series
(edited by Celia Genishi and Donna E. Alvermann), as well as other titles in this series, please visit www.tcpress.com.

JUDITH T. LYSAKER

Before Words

WORDLESS PICTURE BOOKS AND THE DEVELOPMENT OF READING IN YOUNG CHILDREN

FOREWORD BY PETER JOHNSTON

TEACHERS COLLEGE PRESS

TEACHERS COLLEGE | COLUMBIA UNIVERSITY

NEW YORK AND LONDON

Published by Teachers College Press, 1234 Amsterdam Avenue, New York, NY 10027

Library of Congress Cataloging-in-Publication Data

Names: Lysaker, Judith T., author.
Title: Before words : wordless picture books and the development of reading
  in young children / Judith T. Lysaker ; Foreword by Peter Johnston.
Description: New York, NY : Teachers College Press, [2019] I Series: Language
  and literacy series I Includes bibliographical references and index. I
  Identifiers: LCCN 2018038807 (print) I LCCN 2018047943 (ebook) I ISBN
  9780807777008 (ebook) I ISBN 9780807759172 (case) I ISBN 9780807759165
  (pbk.)
Subjects: LCSH: Picture books for children—Educational aspects. I Stories
  without words—Study and teaching (Preschool) I Reading
  comprehension—Study and teaching (Preschool) I Language arts (Preschool)
Classification: LCC LB1044.9.P49 (ebook) I LCC LB1044.9.P49 L97 2019 (print)
  I DDC 371.33/5—dc23
LC record available at https://lccn.loc.gov/2018038807

ISBN 978-0-8077-5916-5 (paper)
ISBN 978-0-8077-5917-2 (hardcover)
ISBN 978-0-8077-7700-8 (ebook)

Printed on acid-free paper
Manufactured in the United States of America

26 25 24 23 22 21 20 19   8 7 6 5 4 3 2 1

For all the children I have been privileged to read with throughout the years.
And in memory of Beth Hopper.

Contents

Foreword

This brilliant and well-researched book is a thoroughly engaging, provocative, and insightful analysis of the process and development of comprehension in young children. Judy Lysaker has solved a problem that has plagued early literacy teachers and researchers for a long time: We have not known how to look at and listen to the processes of children's comprehension—to understand, document, and address their meaning-making in books. Our assessment efforts have focused one way or another on children's knowledge and processing of print. To the extent that we attended to children's meaning-making, retellings and comprehension questions were the best we could come up with, neither of which informs instruction, is interactionally authentic, or leads children to become deeply engaged in sense-making. This book shows us what we have been missing and what to do about it.

I have been waiting for this book, and reading it has changed me. Now I see wordless picture books and the children reading them in an entirely different light. Until now many teachers, while finding such books interesting, had been a bit puzzled as to their value for teaching children to read. Some even thought that a book's lack of words encouraged children to simply make up stories. The author has shown us that making up stories is exactly what children are doing, but that it is also a core process of comprehending that is far from simple. Judy Lysaker has turned wordless books from a curiosity into a powerful learning tool for teachers and children alike.

This book provides a careful empirical and theoretical analysis of examples of children's comprehending processes, with more detailed examples available online for further exploration. Through clear longitudinal and contrasting case studies, the author reveals consistent patterns of development across children and over time, simultaneously revealing the uniqueness of each reader's comprehending processes and trajectory of development. In the process, she reveals the fundamentally relational nature of reading, teaching, and her research. You cannot read this book without being inspired by the depth of her caring about and respect for the children, whose meaning construction she examines so closely. You cannot read this book without recognizing the importance of being present for children, listening to them, and helping them appreciate and expand their experience with books.

In the face of persistently reductionist approaches to young children's reading instruction, this is a wake-up call to those who would diminish young children's playful and imaginative experiences with books and turn them into labor, who would turn an emotionally and relationally laden process into a technical enterprise. Lysaker's research shows how the process of comprehending is also a process of self-construction, of making meaning about the self and others as much as about characters and narratives in the book.

This engaging, insightful book is a particularly valuable resource for researchers and teacher researchers. It provides a nuanced theoretical framework to help us make sense of children's reading behavior. At the same time, it provides concrete strategies for documenting the development of children's comprehending and for responsive teaching to expand that development. It shows why we might choose certain wordless books for particular instructional objectives, and why we might choose certain language in our responses to children's constructions. Additionally, it reveals how we might decide about the timing, function, and context of our use of wordless books. It gives us the tools to notice what is important about children's interactions with books more generally, not just those without words on the page. The author models for us how to respond productively to children's meaning-making with wordless books, with clear explanations of why particular responses are helpful, not only for expanding children's meaning-making resources, but also for expanding the quality of their immediate lives and their humanity.

This book is a breakthrough work. Prepare to have your mind opened to completely new terrain in children's literate development.

—*Peter Johnston*

Acknowledgments

I would like to thank the teachers, principals, and other school leaders who made it possible for me to work with young children in their schools. Without them, this work could not have been done. I also, and especially, want to thank the parents who entrusted their children to me so that we could read together. This was such an enormous gift, for which I am very grateful. I have learned nearly everything from the children. I also wish to thank my colleagues: Peter Johnston and Gay Ivey for their constant and inspiring companionship on my quest to understand reading as human relational activity; Kathleen Martin, for her work on the Head Start project; Christy Wessel Powell, for her invaluable feedback on Noticing Maps; and Melanie Reaves, for her ongoing, generative conversations with me about young children. I am indebted to Emily Spangler at Teachers College Press for her patient and thoughtful handling of this project from its inception and for several helpful conversations across many months, as well as to Lauren Mallett at the Writing Lab at Purdue University for her proofreading of earlier drafts. Finally I want to thank my family, and especially my husband, Paul, for his tireless support and unflinching faith in my work.

CHAPTER 1

Introduction

This is a book about children's readings of wordless books. Children do remarkable things as they read wordless books, before they are able to work with, or in many cases even care to think about, print. As Gordon Wells (1986) noted emphatically, children are meaning-makers. When you put wordless books in children's hands, that meaning-making comes alive because of the qualities and affordances of wordless books and because of the children themselves.

My rationale for writing this book is twofold. First, I hope to extend the current theoretical articulations of emergent reading by providing teachers, teacher educators, literacy researchers, and anyone interested in young children a descriptive and conceptual account of young children's meaning-making during wordless book reading, one that expands the meaningfulness of what comprehending *is* and what it *does* for young children. By conceptualizing and describing young children's comprehending as human meaning-making activity, rather than the execution of skills to achieve prescribed outcomes, I argue that meaning-making with books is both an academic and developmental accomplishment, one in which children not only become readers but develop understandings of themselves and others. Second, I hope to demonstrate that careful observations of children's wordless book readings, and documenting these observations, can be a useful and inspiring way to assess children's meaning-making in a book-related narrative context that informs the kinds of thoughtful response necessary to meaningful literacy instruction for young learners.

I have read wordless books with hundreds of young children over the years, and I have collected, analyzed, sorted, sifted, and studied the narratives children created during those readings. What I have come to discover is that the comprehending activity of 3-, 4-, 5-, and 6-year-olds during wordless book reading is intricate, personal, complex, lively, and intensely relational, and a rich example of a certain kind of human meaning-making. In this book I take a close look at the particular kind of human meaning-making of wordless book reading and examine the specific ways children enact meanings as they read these texts. In that sense, it is a book about emergent reading and specifically about emergent comprehension. However, since it is a book about children's meaning-making, it is also a book about children and how the sense-making they do with books is not just "emergent comprehension" but, for them, a way of being in the world. To sit by a reader and observe all that happens—with their eyes, hands, bodies, and words as they make sense of story—is, to borrow from Lucy Calkins's (2001) description, a small miracle. Where these books provide only images, with stories hinted at and narrative possibilities offered, children author unique texts and something new comes into being every time.

It isn't just the new and often wonderful stories children enact as they read wordless books that fascinate and inspire. The real fascination comes in the activities of comprehending: all that happens when children take books into their hands, explore the world of images laid out before them, and begin to enact and voice meanings with the special symbolic resource of image. At these moments, I feel that I am in the presence of not just an emerging reader, but an emerging person with a growing set of subjectivities that are suddenly visible as the child encounters and chooses to participate in a story world as a new being in that world. Being and becoming are enacted in this time and space we call reading, when sense-making with text—comprehending—is taking hold of a child's consciousness. These are intimate, lovely moments that need to be taken seriously. In the face of highly technical, reductionist definitions of what it means to read and to be a reader, it is important to bring attention to these moments by describing and carefully thinking about what is going on. What happens when children make meaning with books before the onset of decoding, when comprehending is the only thing that matters? How can we think about this early comprehending in ways that break open the complex human experience that it is, lead us to value what children can do, and imagine new ways we can respond?

In this book I attend to these questions and invite you to know children's comprehending in new ways, to participate in this way of making meaning and being in the world with children, and to know children themselves in new ways because their wordless book reading puts you in touch with their sense-making. I hope that this book opens up new ways of understanding and responding to children's reading, as well as providing a different, more person-centered grounding for reading teaching and research. Finally, I hope this book helps you reconsider reading comprehension and what it means for the young children in your own lives. Because this book is about children and their meaning-making experiences with text, the specific activities that children use in making sense of storied worlds, and how interested adults might respond to those activities, I think anyone interested in enhancing children's experiences with narrative texts will find something for them in this book.

An aside about terminology before beginning: You will notice that I purposefully use the word *comprehending* to denote activity, rather than the more common term *comprehension*, a noun. I do this to highlight the fact that I attend exclusively to *what children are doing* as they read. You might also notice that I use the word *activity* rather than *strategy*. Strategy denotes a kind of purposeful application of something, in this case ways of comprehending, to achieve a particular outcome. While young children's meaning-making is purposeful in itself (like all human meaning-making) their ways of sense-making, rather than being strategically enacted, happen as organic to their sense-making.

My interest in this book is entirely in children's activity with and within storied worlds as enacted during wordless book reading—their independent comprehending work. In the spirit of Rosenblatt (2004) and Iser (1978), I take the position that *meaning* is "what happens" during reading and offer a detailed view of what is happening when young children read wordless books. I outline a set of comprehending activities that constitute their meaning-making and suggest that our observations and assessments of young children's comprehending should examine and value their comprehending activity, rather than what they take away from reading, or what Aukerman (2013) calls "comprehension as outcome." In fact, I purposefully omit what many might consider *comprehension*; that is, specific knowledge children take away from the reading or what questions they might be able to answer. Many other books attend to that view of comprehension. By focusing on "what happens" as children read narrative wordless books, I make a shift away from thinking about young children's comprehension from an efferent view and move toward a more aesthetic one (Rosenblatt, 2004). An efferent perspective on comprehension notes and values what readers take away from texts, while an aesthetic one notes and values the *experience* of sense-making itself.

Paying attention to the experience and activity of comprehending is particularly appropriate when examining children's understating of story because making sense of stories is like making sense of life; comprehending involves understanding ourselves, other people, and relationships, and taps on deeply personal aspects of being (Ivey & Johnston, 2016; Lysaker & Nie, 2017). Perhaps more importantly, a focus on comprehending as activity or experience makes it possible to notice *how* children arrive at understandings. Noticing these activities of personal sense-making allows teachers, parents, and other interested adults to respond in ways that enhance and promote children's developing capacities for comprehending text. I introduce the use of *Noticing Maps,* blank assessment forms that I have created for use during observations, to facilitate noticing and responding to young children's comprehending, and suggest that being with young children in side-by-side wordless book reading is a useful context in which to observe and respond to the specific ways in which children make sense in storied worlds.

WHY WORDLESS BOOK READING?

As we will see, wordless books offer children open spaces for sense-making, spaces full of possibility in which their emerging comprehending capacities can develop. There are many reasons why this kind of meaning-making experience with books is important for young children. First, the need to provide children open spaces in the curriculum for personal, creative, and imaginative literacy engagement has increased over the recent past. The prevalence of high-stakes testing, in kindergarten and beyond, has had the effect of narrowing and pressurizing the literacy curriculum and upping the ante for young children. (Dudley-Marling, 2013; Dyson, 2015). Understandably, teachers who are anxious to have students do well on standardized tests often spend a good deal of their time teaching and assessing what children need to know to be test-takers, leaving little time for responding to individual children's meaning-making. Since most standardized tests do not represent a broad or current view of reading, children get the diet of skills and subskills instruction that is assessed by tests. Accordingly, the time for activities that foster imaginative, creative, and constructive capacities is reduced.

Related to the narrowing of curriculum is the relatively new expectation that kindergartners will leave kindergarten reading. One result of this expectation is an intense curricular focus on decoding, often beginning in preschool classrooms. Making sure that children become efficient decoders—in combination with the steady diet of "little books" in popular core reading programs—means that a majority of children's reading time is spent on books with contrived language and constrained purposes. Decoding and literal understandings of simple text are the key objectives, making teachers monitors of children's subskill and text-based achievements. Time for thoughtful response to children's personal sense-making is limited and, for teachers, may even seem nonexistent. Beyond this, books themselves take on a narrowed meaning, which can shape young children's thinking about what books are, and what reading is. As Bomer (2013) points out, books can become objects to practice with, not experiences to be savored. While it may be argued that simple books with contrived language and the skills-oriented instruction they are used for have some place in classrooms where children are learning to read, such books significantly reduce opportunities for children to engage in their own meaning-making. However, wordless books, as we will see, are often more complex texts and, because of the absence of print, invite and encourage the experience of personal sense-making.

Perhaps the most damaging result of the narrowed curriculum is that the ways a child can succeed have become limited (Dyson, 2015). Both the content and entry points into the curriculum are predetermined by the test and curriculum authors, and are not necessarily connected to children's backgrounds, interests, or wonderings. Children are not able to express and enact the intricacies of their own experiences and unique capacities for meaning-making within a restrictive curriculum. As Dyson points out, it is important to notice that children do not feel this kind of restriction uniformly. The more closely matched children's experiences and identities are with what is required by the curriculum, the less constraining it is. Because those of privilege create most standard assessments and literacy core programs, the constraints experienced by those of less privilege, including many children of color, children who are poor, or children who are new to English can be profound indeed. The relationship between these children and the curriculum is distant and foreign, making possibilities for engaging in rich, lively experiences difficult to attain (Lysaker, 2012).

A renewed focus on standards has also contributed to the narrowing of curricula for young children. The Common Core State Standards have been adopted in 41 states, and the implementation of these standards has several implications for young children. The text-focused, analytic nature of the reading standards positions children as merely consumers of others' ideas (Bomer, 2013). They are expected to determine an author's meanings and rationally defend this determination by referring back to the text. The notion that comprehending can be a personal, social, and lived experience is absent. As Bomer puts it, from this perspective, "A novel is never simply a world to get lost in, or a journey of self-discovery, or an experience of beauty and insight" (p. 31). On the face of it, the lack of regard for reading as personal experience may seem relatively unimportant in the early years of schooling. After all, learning the code and figuring out that an author is saying *something*—and something that you can figure out—is important if you are 3, 4, 5, or 6 years old. However, regularly positioning children as consumers rather than as meaning-makers can change how young children think about themselves and their roles, skills, and possibilities as readers.

Wordless book reading also helps meet some current challenges facing the field of literacy. First, it is important to know as much as possible about young children's very early burgeoning comprehending abilities in book contexts (Dooley & Mathews, 2009) since these early capacities will be drawn on in children's later print reading. Second, we need more ways to authentically assess these abilities prior to print reading (Duke & Carlisle, 2011). Assessment of comprehending is less attended to than assessment of subskills considered related to later successful print reading, such as phonological and phonemic awareness, alphabet knowledge, and phonics, which continue to dominate emergent reading assessment. For example, the Phonological Awareness Literacy Screening (PALS), as the name implies, addresses only phonological awareness, a child's ability to segment and blend sounds heard in words (see website at palsresource.info/assessments). The Northwest Evaluation Association (NWEA) has a reading fluency assessment for K–3 readers that measures reading fluency and decoding accuracy (see website at www.nwea.org). Dynamic Indicators of Basic Literacy Skills (DIBELS) measures phonemic awareness, alphabetic principle, accuracy, and fluency (see dibels.org/DIBELS_Next_Info.pdf). DIBELS also has subtests for preschoolers, called Preschool Evaluation Literacy Indicators (PELI) that include alphabet knowledge, vocabulary, oral language, and phonemic awareness (see dibels.org/PELI_Early_Release_Fact_Sheet.pdf).

Though both NWEA and DIBELS include comprehension assessments, these consist of asking questions of children as they read (NWEA) or hear (DIBELS) a story. These questions are often literal and text-based, getting at only what children take away from the text in terms of right answers to predetermined questions and not the ways in which they make meaning. DIBELS also has an assessment that claims to measure comprehension as part of oral reading fluency. In 1st through 3rd grades, children are asked to retell a story and "try to tell everything" they can (Goodman, 2006, p. 84). The retelling score is based on the number of words they use in the retelling excluding any repetitions of places where the retelling is unrelated to the text read (Goodman, 2006). For preschool children, DIBELS has a cloze-style retelling component during which the assessor retells the story leaving out words that the child is expected to fill in. While the ability to retell using many words, answer questions, or fill in the blanks can provide some information about what children know about a story after they read or hear it, these measures are limited and tell us virtually nothing about *how* children achieve any understandings that might be apparent through these measures. Even some wordless book reading assessments tend to examine more discrete text- and language-based aspects of children's readings, such as the syntactic complexity of children's sentences, vocabulary, references to story elements, or match between text images and children's narrations (Paris & Paris, 2003). While analysis of these elements of wordless book reading can shed light on language and vocabulary development as well as children's abilities to represent literal meanings in speech (i.e., story elements), like print-related assessments, they don't tell us much about *how* children are making meaning during reading.

Using language-based subskills assessments of young children's reading comprehension can also be problematic. Children whose oral language may not reflect the syntactic structures and vocabulary of Standard American English, such as those with dialect differences or English learners, are further marginalized by assessments that don't represent what they *do* to make meaning. More inclusive, socially just avenues for assessment of reading are needed (Willis, 2008). As we will see in coming chapters, wordless books offer an open-ended space for meaning-making with less constrained entry points and more possibilities for teachers and others to observe, value, and nurture children's personal sense-making.

THEORETICAL CONSIDERATIONS

In this book I frame what comprehending is and how it happens with ideas about the dialogic, relational nature of human beingness (Bakhtin, 1981; Buber, 1970; Heidegger, 1953) and human meaning-making (Linell, 2009; Trevarthen, 2009; Vygotsky, 1978; Zittoun, 2006). Like all of us, young children are always and inherently in the condition of both being in and desiring relationships. When children succeed in seeking out and forming relationships that work well—including, in my view, relationships with text—they thrive. Without these relationships, they suffer. Within rich relational worlds, both real and storied, children participate in the dynamic relational inside-out, and outside-in, bidirectional cultivation of personhood. Their language, their minds, their very selves develop a kind of relational beingness through social interaction (Vygotsky, 1978). This ever-evolving relationality is a dynamic resource for sense-making in children's lives, both in their actual everyday social worlds and within the vicarious social worlds of story.

Comprehending as Relational

If as human beings we are relational, then it follows that young children enter and make sense of storied worlds as relational beings. They dialogically engage with characters as vicarious others as part of sense-making (Lysaker, Tonge, Gauson, & Miller, 2011). The relationality of children's comprehending is particularly salient in their reading of narrative texts since stories are symbolically represented peopled worlds. Like actual peopled worlds, stories offer relational invitations to enter, connect with, and make sense of human experience. As a central part of sense-making, children recontextualize their experiences within narrative worlds to form relationships with the characters they meet. Using their own recontextualized experiences and relational histories, they imagine what characters are like, what they are thinking and feeling, and what their worlds are like. When children are comprehending, they listen, respond, and participate in vicarious social worlds where they can feel joy, comfort, tension, or conflict. In Chapter 3 we will see children actively using their bodies—hands, voices, gaze—in these sense-making experiences. Children's comprehending with texts is a relational meaning-making event, one in which children's ongoing relationality and all that constitutes that relationality is both resource and outcome.

Louise Rosenblatt wrote extensively about readers' relationships with text in her transactional theory. She claims, "There is no generic reader or generic text" (1983, p. 25), but only the dynamic relationships—what she terms "transactions"—between particular readers and particular texts. In narrative reading, like children's wordless book readings in this book,

Rosenblatt argues, readers attend to what is "lived through" in the reading experience:

> The aesthetic reader pays attention to—savors—the qualities of the feelings, ideas, situations, scenes, personalities, and emotions that are called forth and participates in the tensions, conflicts, and resolutions of the images, ideas, and scenes as they unfold. (2004, p. 1373)

When readers pay attention to and savor the human life of the narrative world, when they enact meanings as they participate in that world, they are *comprehending*.

Bruner (1986) makes the claim that narrative consists of two landscapes: one of action and one of consciousness. The landscape of action naturally consists of the human events of the story and what is happening. The landscape of consciousness consists of the "inner worlds" of characters: what they believe and what they are thinking, feeling, or wondering. The landscapes of action and consciousness help define the human, relational worlds that children encounter in story. If we pay attention, the landscape of consciousness tells us why the landscape of action unfolds as it does. In Chapters 4 and 5 we will see children pay attention to the human life of narrative worlds as part of comprehending, recontextualizing their experiences, and imagining the inner worlds and lives of characters. In Chapter 6 we will see that children's agile dialogic movement around the landscapes of consciousness and action contribute to their sense-making.

Texts as Relational Spaces

Throughout this book it is assumed that narrative texts, in particular, function as relational spaces, dialogic contexts of peopled, storied worlds where readers can participate relationally in the ongoing dialogue between voices and positions of subjectivities represented in word and image (Lysaker et al., 2011; Popova, 2015). Thinking about texts as active participants in children's sense-making requires a shift in how we think about text. Texts can serve as dialogic objects to participate with, rather than static ones to be figured out (Bertau, 2007; Zittoun, 2006). From this perspective I suggest that texts are a particular kind of participation genre and a way of being with others intersubjectively (Fuchs & De Jaegher, 2009). Viewing texts as dialogic objects and participation genres that represent human experience through the presentation of multiple interacting subjectivities highlights their dynamic qualities. Consequently, narrative texts are lively, relational contexts within which readers meet and form relationships with others as they are "addressed" by the subjectivities of the text *as* comprehending activity. While comprehending narrative texts, readers listen, enact, and respond to the text's characters and narrators, and form intricate, dynamic, and intersubjective webs of relation (Lysaker & Arvelo Alicea, 2017; Popova, 2015).

Of course, children's relationships during reading are not precisely the same as those they have in the actual world. Relationships constructed during reading are less direct, one step removed from actual experience. In order to comprehend and form relationships with and within storied worlds, children have to link their personal sense-making (situated within their relational experiences) with the cultural symbols represented in text. The connections children make between personal and cultural meanings do not exist prior to meaning-making (Zittoun, 2015). Rather, particular readers in dialogue with particular texts imagine them during comprehending (Lysaker & Wessel-Powell, in press; Zittoun, 2015.) In Chapter 4 we will see that creating these imaginative connections between the personal (me) and the cultural (text) involve the comprehending activities of response, recognition, and recontextualization.

We don't often think about imagination in relation to the sense-making children do during reading. Instead, we tend to think of imagination as a somewhat charming part of childhood play. Though parents and teachers take delight in children's imaginative activity and psychologists recognize its role in children's' development, we often leave out the potential importance of imagination in reading. However, imagination is what makes the dialogic encounter within storied worlds possible. It is the basis of any relational activity with and within text, and is therefore integral to comprehending. As Bakhtin (1981) suggests in the title of his well-known work *The Dialogic Imagination*, imagination is central to the dialogic nature of meaning-making itself, and particularly within the world of story. Imagination lands children in the storied world, a new relational space available to them through the material of books. We will see children use both social and narrative imagination to make sense of story in Chapter 5.

QUALITIES OF WORDLESS BOOKS

I turn now from theory to talk about wordless books as the context within which the theory just outlined is applied to children's emergent comprehending. To understand deeply and more specifically how wordless book reading can be an important comprehending experience for children—and how those readings can serve as important artifacts of that understanding for teachers and researchers—we need to look carefully at just what wordless books are. While it may be obvious to say that wordless books are books without words, I think it can be helpful to describe what not having words means, as it pertains to the composition of the text and what the reader does with it.

What does it mean to be *wordless*? This is a question with many different answers. While some define *wordless books* as those with minimal

linguistic text beyond what is included in elements like title, author, illustrators, and so forth. My own assessment of wordlessness is slightly different.
In my work with children as young as 3 years old, I have found that the
presence of even some words alters their stance toward the reading. They
become concerned with the words: "If they are on this page, why are they
not on that page?" "What does the word say?" "I can't read this." In many
cases, children's preoccupation with words takes away from their willingness to engage deeply in sense-making with the images before them, and
therefore constrains their sense of agency and confidence as readers. I have
accordingly chosen to work with children using books that are completely wordless. By this I mean that no aspect of the story is communicated
through printed linguistic text. There may be words used in the title or
endpapers, but the story itself appears in images only.

Wordlessness influences children's comprehending. Rendering meanings
only in image enhances the addressivity of the text. *Addressivity*, according
to Bakhtin (1986) is "the quality of turning to someone" (p. 99). In applying
this term to wordless book reading, I am suggesting that images "turn to"
readers in a way that is particularly recognizable by young children, and
therefore invites them into dialogic engagement. Unlike linguistically represented meanings, which are abstract and require decoding, image-only texts
represent story meanings and characters (i.e., meanings about people) in
shape, line, and color. With the exception of their two-dimensionality, these
renderings of meaning resemble the actual world. This rendering enhances
the addressivity of texts, particularly for young children, because it makes
characters more present as human beings and allows readers to make connections via "sensitive contact" (Bertau, 2014) that enriches and enlivens
readers' relationships with text (Lysaker, 2014).

Wordless Books as Complex Texts

Regardless, or perhaps because of their image-only quality, wordless books
are often complex texts. Several literacy scholars have studied the genre of
wordless books. It is not my purpose to provide a complete genre analysis
here. However, describing the complexity of wordless books as a kind of
text is important to understanding wordless book reading as "real" reading.
Along with others who are interested in wordless books (Arizpe, Colomer,
& Martinez-Roldan, 2014: Crawford & Hade, 2000; Serafini, 2014), I
have identified the qualities that contribute to their complexity and to the
meaning-making demands they make of young readers. One such quality
is *ambiguity;* no single, certain meaning is readily apparent (Arizpe et al.
2014; Lysaker & Miller, 2012). While narrative texts also have a set of
variable meanings, wordlessness adds to this ambiguity. Without at least
the surface-level precision of the words to suggest a first, literal layer of
meaning, readers are required to tolerate and make sense of the multiple

potential meanings represented by image. This ambiguity continues across narrative time and asks readers to work with these meanings in relation to one another. Arizpe et al. (2014) argue that this requires readers to choose a "narrative path" from several possible pathways and make subsequent decisions that build a coherent narrative along that pathway. Another quality of many wordless books that contributes to their complexity as texts is that they are crafted into separate *episodes*. Like comic strips and graphic novels, wordless books often feature frames created by the illustrator that place boundaries around events. As readers follow these framed meanings, they encounter gaps in time and place, and things left unexplained. Narrative gaps ask readers to connect episodes into a larger, coherent meaning using their imaginations (Iser, 1978; Lysaker & Miller, 2012).

Beyond making sense of images, readers of wordless books must recast these meanings into spoken narrative, using what is available to them in their oral language stores. Taking meanings constructed from images and representing them in oral language is not simple. Reading images, and voicing their meanings in speech, requires translating meanings from one language mode to another, or *transmediation* (Suhor, 1984). Transmediation has been theorized and studied primarily by researchers interested in how children move their understandings from written or oral language to visual modes (Albers & Harste, 2007; Leland & Harste, 1994). For example, a child making sense of a story through drawing can explore those meanings differently because the medium of paper and crayon affords particular expressive possibilities tied to the medium's materiality. Line, color, and shape allow the exploration and expression of meaning in a way that linguistic resources do not. Such meanings can expand and deepen as the language user navigates multiple modes. This generativity constitutes a particular kind of creative activity. Just as imagination is used to link personal and cultural meanings, "the connection between the two sign systems must be *invented* [emphasis added], as the connection does not exist prior to the act of transmediation itself," (Siegel, 1995, p. 463). The work of transmediation affords new meaning-making possibilities because of the reader's move across modes and the demands of this complex, creative, and thinking–feeling language work. Making sense of and responding to images, choices, and thoughts with a set of coherent meanings in linear speech via transmediation is an important and often overlooked comprehending activity of young children.

Wordless Books as Contexts for Assessment

As I move forward from this broad, person-centered view of comprehending to argue that the observation of this transformative, beautiful act can be richly informative as an assessment tool, I feel some hesitation. Whenever we observe, record, gather up, and make sense of what children do—that is, informally assess their activity—we run the risk of synthesizing and summarizing too soon, checking the boxes for what we've seen, assigning numbers to what we've observed, and contributing to the current and destructive reductionist project. It is tempting to grab onto something that feels immediately and concretely helpful in order to meet the accountability requirements we all face. However, we can resist. In the hands of teachers, the observation of wordless book readings can be rich, living information that is put to good use in classrooms. If we think of children's comprehending as the *activity* of making meaning with books, then how children read wordless books is an excellent context for observing that activity. From a transactional perspective, wordless book readings are living artifacts of the reader–text transaction (Rosenblatt, 2004) and can show us how readers engage in and enact that transaction.

Much like the writing samples of young children, which serve as dynamic artifacts of their writing processes, wordless book readings can inform teachers and researchers about comprehending processes. As Harste, Woodward, and Burke (1984), Shagoury (2008), Wood Ray (2004), and many others have demonstrated, children's writing samples are valued for what they tell us about children's knowledge of print, the world, their composing processes, and where they situate themselves as encoders, social agents, cultural participants, and imaginative meaning-makers. Though talking with children about their writing is eminently helpful, writing samples offer an intricate and useful representation of children's individual transactions with their own emerging texts. All of this is present in the approximations they make as they compose.

Wordless book readings can function in similar ways. As artifacts of children's emergent comprehending, wordless book readings show us the meaning-making aspects of their individual transactions with text, which otherwise can be difficult to identify. In Chapter 7 I introduce Noticing Maps as a way to document the comprehending activities of children during wordless book reading. Noticing Maps, as the name implies, are intended as tools for mapping the topography of specific comprehending activities as they occur during wordless book reading. Cartographers create map topographies to visually represent the surface level of the earth and map out what can be directly observed. Topographic maps of the earth do not tell the whole story, however. They do not describe what lies under the surface, or even how the surface came to be as it is. They provide hints, which can be useful when carefully interpreted.

Noticing Maps serve as a means of guiding observations and making note of the "surface features" of children's comprehending as it unfolds during wordless book reading: its high points, valleys, shapes, and textures. As professionals, we can observe and interpret children's wordless book readings to ascertain the strengths of their personal sense-making as well as aspects of comprehending that are not yet developed. In this book we will notice, document, and respond to several features of young children's comprehending activity: (1) how they orchestrate meanings from image to speech; (2) how they use their bodies to enact meanings within storied worlds; (3) how they respond, recognize, and recontextualize experience; (4) how they use social and narrative imagination to make sense of the landscapes of consciousness and action at play in storied worlds; and (5) how they use fluency in terms of prosody and dialogic agility to traverse those landscapes as part of meaning-making. These activities of comprehending, which will be thoroughly described in later chapters, are demonstrated by young children prior to their ability to read print, and are key aspects of later comprehension of printed narrative texts. All readers orchestrate meaning by searching, cross-checking, and self-correcting. All readers of story have initial personal responses to the narrative world, recognize their own lives there or find contrasts to them, and recontexualize their own experiences in order to comprehend. Readers of print texts also need to imagine the inner worlds of characters through social imagination and create their own understandings of how narratives unfold using narrative imagination. Finally, accomplished readers voice and listen to characters (Bomer, 2006) as they read and navigate landscapes of consciousness and action with dialogic agility. Wordless book reading therefore provides an unusual opportunity for observing and nurturing comprehending activities needed for later reading of books with words before, and in some cases well before, young children are facile with printed text.

As suggested earlier in this chapter, it is critical for teachers and other interested adults to know how children make sense of text, since activity, including the activities of comprehending, is where learning is happening and is therefore the source of authentic and effective instruction. Supporting and nurturing young children's reading involves sensitive observation of their comprehending as it happens and careful responses that serve to help children develop their personal sense-making. In this spirit, each chapter includes descriptions of possible reading conversations that teachers could have with young readers. Such conversations, as well as other instructional responses, are feasible only after keen observation of children's wordless book reading, which can be facilitated through the use of Noticing Maps. For thinking through what a reading conversation might be like, I suggest teachers consider these questions: What is the goal of my conversation with the child? How will what I lead this child forward into more complex, enjoyable, and rich participation with and within storied worlds? As Peter Johnston (2004) reminds us, the words we use matter and how we talk to young children about their reading is critically important, as it will help shape how they think about reading and who they are as readers.

There is much to discover and contemplate in close observation and analysis of children's wordless book readings. Wordless book readings are rich artifacts of the lively relationships that constitute children's meaning-making transactions with and within texts that can inform how we teach and how we talk with children, as well as transform how we think about young children's comprehending. However, their wordless book readings are also literacy artifacts of the creative and imaginative engagement of their enacted subjectivities and, like other stories people tell, can be appreciated as important artifacts of their developing identities (Lysaker & Miller, 2012).

THE CHILDREN, SCHOOLS, AND CLASSROOMS

The children whose readings fill these pages come from two different school contexts. One of these contexts is a set of early learning centers in an urban setting. The other is a Head Start preschool in a different urban setting. All of the readers we encounter are 3, 4, 5, or 6 years old and represent different ethnic and racial backgrounds. All spoke English as their first language, and some spoke with dialect features common to African American English.

None of the children we meet in this book were reading conventionally at the time of these readings. Only James was beginning to decode print independently. James is also the only child who attended a school with a low rate of free or reduced-price lunches, indicating a population of relative advantage. All the other children we meet in these chapters were living without economic advantage, attending either a Head Start preschool or an early learning center with a high rate of free or reduced-price lunches. I visited all the classrooms in the schools our readers attended. Each of these children was fortunate to be in a classroom where literacy was greatly valued by dedicated and caring teachers.

The literacy curriculum of the early learning centers was based on the workshop approach to reading and writing (Calkins, 1994, 2001). The children were engaged in literacy minilessons as well as independent reading and writing from the first day of kindergarten. Guided reading groups were a regular practice and wordless books were not an instructional focus. The Head Start preschool also had a vibrant literacy program with interactive reading and writing, read-alouds, and opportunities for children to choose and read books independently or collaboratively with their peers. At the time that I read with the preschool children, their Head Start teachers were participating in professional development with me that focused on comprehending.

The children in these chapters demonstrate a range of comprehending activity and often differ significantly in how they go about sense-making with texts. As a researcher who has worked with many children beyond those we meet in this book, it is apparent to me that there are trends in how comprehending develops in young children as it is enacted in wordless book reading. However, these trends, which I will describe later in Chapter 7, are not stages or developmental rules. If we regarded them as such, children would surely defy them! We will meet a 3-year-old who is so present to and active in story as a meaning-maker it seems as though she might just leap right into the pages. We will meet a 6-year-old who appears the opposite, hesitant, as if holding back. This should not be surprising, since we know that children's invisible time-layered experiences with language and reading have a lot to do with what they choose to do when they meet up with a book. This means that children will very likely jumble up any developmental trajectory we may want to create or settle into. With this in mind, I will cautiously comment on the patterns I have observed in their comprehending of wordless books in Chapter 7.

Some notes on process: The wordless book readings you will encounter in the pages of this book were generated in two ways. Our kindergarten readers read *I Had Measles* in quiet spaces outside their classrooms as part of a research project on children's development of social imagination. It was the only text available to them for this reading. This is important to note since offering children choices has the advantage of increasing children's engagement by giving them some ownership over the reading (Cambourne, 1995). The kindergarteners we meet in this book did not have this advantage, yet most were nonetheless happy to read with me.

Our preschoolers read with me at what we called the "Reading Table." I set up the Reading Table in the hall just outside one of the preschool classrooms and had my collection of wordless books spread out on the table so the children could choose what they would like to read. Many children considered a chance to read at the Reading Table as something special. Nearly all the wordless book readings occurred in a context I refer to as "side-by-side" reading. I sat beside the children and looked at the book with them much as parents do when reading with young children. However, we did not explore the book together page by page talking about the images, as you might for other purposes. Rather, my rule of thumb was to participate only when the children requested it, either verbally or through their actions, so that I could observe their independent sense-making and not disrupt their unfolding narratives. In this way, side-by-side wordless book reading is somewhat like taking a running record. The purpose is to be present to and observe all that is happening as the child reads.

WORDLESS BOOKS READ BY CHILDREN IN THIS BOOK

The wordless books used by children in the subsequent chapters were all part of a collection of wordless books for young children I created by looking specifically for wordless books meant for younger readers that were commercially available. As mentioned earlier, with the exception of *I Had Measles*, children's choices resulted in the use of these particular books from that collection. In Chapter 8 I offer some thoughts on how to build a wordless book library of your own. You can find the full bibliographic information in theAppendix . I also provide transcripts of each child's reading and page-by-page descriptions of each book alongside the children's narrations in the online resources for this book, available at www.tcpress.com.

I Had Measles **by The Wright Group (1987).** When I first began using wordless books with children several years ago, I came across *I Had Measles*, a wordless book (now out of print) that was written for parents to read with their young children. Though the book is out of date and limited in its stereotypical depiction of a family (white, two parents of different genders, and two children), it nonetheless has other qualities that make it interesting and relevant to most of the children who have read it with me. One quality is the family context. The story is about a child who is sick and the ways in which the family takes care of her. The sick child appears to be female, and there is another younger child who appears to be a boy, giving readers of both genders opportunities for identification. *I Had Measles* features soft pastel illustrations that depict characters ambiguously and story events episodically. As mentioned earlier, presenting a story in episodes often creates time gaps that invite imaginative comprehending activities. In its peopled story world, *I Had Measles* has five other unnamed human characters, a dog, and some stuffed animals. In some ways this is the most complex of the wordless books I have used with young children because of the number of characters, possible relationships, range of emotions, and frequent time gaps.

Breakfast for Jack **by Pat Schories (2004).** *Breakfast for Jack* is also set in a family context. It is morning and a family is getting ready for their day. A woman and male child appear in the first pages along with a cat and a dog named Jack, the main character. The story revolves around the idea that Jack is hungry, wants to be fed, and is worried that he won't be. In fact, the family leaves the house without feeding him, but the boy remembers at the last minute and returns to feed him. One of the challenges young readers face in *Breakfast for Jack* is the representation of a sequence of events with the same characters on a single page. This manipulation of characters in narrative time, like time gaps, is an interpretive challenge.

When Jack Goes Out **by Pat Schories (2010).** *When Jack Goes Out* is another book in the series about Jack by Pat Schories. In this story Jack goes out to his dog house to settle down for the night. However, some unexpected visitors appear in a spaceship. The space visitors unhook Jack's leash and the adventures begin. *When Jack Goes Out* features Jack and the space visitors as the central characters. *When Jack Goes Out* has several time gaps for readers' imaginative comprehending. In addition, the illustrator does not depict Jack's family, with the exception of the boy, who plays a small role, and one other family member who is barely visible through the window of the family's house. This omission contributes to the ambiguity of the text.

Float by Daniel Miyares (2015). *Float* is the story of a little boy who makes a paper boat and takes it outside with him on a rainy day. The story unfolds as the boy watches his boat float through puddles and down a drain. *Float* presents several challenges. Like *Breakfast for Jack*, sequences of events, instead of single events, are sometimes depicted on the same page. In addition, there are time gaps during which the scene changes. *Float* features one child (presumably a boy) as the central character and an adult male (presumably the father) who has a small role at the beginning and end of the story. The appeal and challenge of *Float* for young readers is the adventure of the boat itself, with its twists, turns, and dramatic moments.

Wave by Suzy Lee (2008). This wordless book, illustrated with watercolors in soft shades of blues, depicts a little girl's visit to the beach. Her adventure includes playing with the waves as they come and go on the sand. The girl is the main human character and an adult female plays a minor role. In *Wave*, the wave itself serves as a second main character. The interaction between the child and the wave appeals to children and provides comprehending challenges since children have to imagine the wave as a character and follow the girl's changing relationship with it.

WHAT TO EXPECT IN THIS BOOK

Following this introduction, Chapters 2–6 are each devoted to an aspect of children's comprehending. These distinctions are in some ways artificial since children's meaning-making is experienced holistically. However, I disentangle what I can for the purposes of illustrating the importance of each aspect, as well as aiding in their documentation. We meet at least two children in each chapter and get to know their wordless book readings.

Chapter 2 deals with the idea of orchestration in children's wordless book reading, particularly how they make meaning across the modes of word and image. In Chapter 3 I focus on the ways in which children use their bodies to place themselves in relation to texts as part of their comprehending. Chapters 4 and 5 deal more specifically with the relational activities of comprehending. Chapter 4 focuses on response, recognition, and recontextualization, while Chapter 5 examines how young readers use social imagination and narrative imagination and enact intersubjective relationships as critical components of comprehending. We shift our attention to fluency in Chapter 6 in order to examine children's use of prosody and dialogic agility to comprehend narrative worlds.

Chapter 7, "Wordless Book Reading as Assessment," differs from the preceding five chapters. In this chapter I introduce Noticing Maps and demonstrate how I use Noticing Maps to document children's comprehending during wordless book reading. I demonstrate how Noticing Maps can be used as tools to examine children's comprehending during one-time individual readings, to compare children's readings of different texts, or to compare their readings of the same text at different points in time. In Chapter 8 I situate side-by-side wordless book reading in the larger contexts of early childhood curriculum and suggest ways of building a classroom wordless book library.

CHAPTER 2

Comprehending as Orchestration Across Modes

I now begin a series of chapters in which we turn to children and their wordless book readings to examine the set of comprehending activities outlined in Chapter 1. In this chapter I examine the ways in which young children orchestrate images as they read wordless books, and I highlight the specific challenge of *transmediation*—orchestrating meaning across language modes—as an integral aspect of comprehending wordless books. I start with examining the orchestration of meanings across modes because it is integral to the act of wordless book reading itself and can be seen in every child's rendition of a wordless text.

We meet 3-year-old Hallie and 6-year-olds Chloe and Maya to see how young children orchestrate across the modes of image and speech as well as bring them together to construct narratives during wordless book reading. We will consider specific aspects of orchestration that can be documented for the purposes of engaging children in reading conversations about their comprehending.

TRANSMEDIATION: MOVING FROM IMAGE TO ORAL NARRATION

A noted in Chapter 1, wordless books are often complex texts that present several meaning-making demands. Wordless books are ambiguous, and without the surface level certainty of words to read, young children are asked to make sense of multiple indefinite meanings and choose a "narrative path" among many (Arizpe, Colomer, & Martínez-Roldán, 2014). As readers create this path they are also required to orchestrate meanings that are often bounded by frames and suggest gaps in time and place, and to transmediate these meanings from image into spoken narrative.

Apprehending meanings in images and recasting them in oral language is complex work. Reading images involves responding to their particular *addressivities,* the ways in which the images "turn to" readers, inviting them into dialogic engagement. Readers transact dialogically with the text and coauthor new meanings as they put together their personal experiences with the text world in meaningful ways (Rosenblatt, 2004). These new meanings must then must be articulated in speech. Voicing the meanings that constitute the dialogue between reader and text requires the *transmediation*, or "moving," of those meanings from one language mode to another (Suhor, 1984). Meanings can expand and deepen as a consequence of this movement. After all, meaning in one mode does not simply and equally stand for meaning in another (Siegel, 1995). Rather, meanings constructed by readers in response to image are re-created as they are spoken because of the necessity to represent and enact them linguistically. In wordless book reading the transmediation of meanings is a critical part of comprehending. Reading and responding to images, making choices, forming thoughts, and enacting a coherent set of meanings in linear speech via transmediation is a challenging, important, often overlooked comprehending activity of young children.

The ways in which images appear on the pages of books is important to how children read wordless books. The characteristics of image—salience, positioning, use of color and vectors (invisible lines implied between images)—contribute to children's comprehending activity during wordless book reading (Lysaker & Miller, 2012; Serafini, 2010). *Salience*, the relative importance of different images or aspects of image, is a particularly important characteristic of image. Salience is what often draws readers' gaze. Artists achieve salience through positioning, foregrounding, backgrounding, color, and so on. In this chapter I will refer to some of these characteristics as they apply to children's comprehending activity. (For a broader discussion about reading images, see Kress & van Leeuwen, 1996. For a more in-depth look at reading images during wordless book reading, see Lysaker & Miller, 2012, and Serafini, 2010.)

As readers do the work of transmediation and navigate the ambiguities of wordless texts, they orchestrate meanings in ways that are similar to what others have noticed as readers work with printed texts (Clay, 1991; Goodman, Watson, & Burke, 1987). For example, using rereading or repetition to gain momentum, pausing and hesitating in order to think, cross-checking meanings across modes, and self-correcting when meanings aren't working together are ways in which young children do the complicated, messy work of orchestrating meanings across the modes of wordless book reading (Lysaker & Hopper, 2015). These activities illustrate the details of children's orchestrating and help us see important parallels between wordless book reading and later proficient print reading.

HALLIE, CHLOE, AND MAYA

At age 3, Hallie is the youngest of our three readers. Hallie is mixed-race and was in her first year at the Head Start preschool when she read *Breakfast for Jack* with me. Hallie came to the Reading Table quietly with eyes lowered, appearing quite shy, yet surprised me with her eagerness to read—she read three books in our time together! Chloe and Maya are both White and in their kindergarten year at the Early Learning Centers. (For more on Chloe's and Maya's readings, see Lysaker & Hopper, 2015.) Chloe had turned 6 just a month prior to her reading of *I Had Measles*. She was eager to read and appeared confident. Our third reader, Maya, was also 6 when she read *I Had Measles* with me. Maya approached the reading with a quiet seriousness. As a reminder, *Breakfast for Jack* is about a dog who is not fed breakfast as a busy family leaves for the day. *I Had Measles* is a story of a child who is sick with measles whose family cares for her. A more complete description of the books can be found in Chapter 1, a bibliography of titles in the Appendix, and full transcripts of children's readings can be found in the online resources for this chapter (see online Appendixes 2.A, 2.B, and 2.C, available at www.tcpress.com).

Hallie's Orchestration Across Modes

As Hallie sits to read with me, she chooses books quickly beginning with *Pancakes for Breakfast* (dePaola, 1978) and moving to *Breakfast for Jack*. Though appearing timid, she seems to know how to read a book with someone and find quiet pleasure in it. I ask her if she has read *Breakfast for Jack* before, and she shakes her head "no."

As I open *Breakfast for Jack*, Hallie's eyes scan the pages curiously. At the title page Hallie begins reading softly, and I have to lean in to hear her read, "The dog's crying." She turns the page, looks to the left and reads, "The kitty is climbing up," then pauses and reads, "Somebody's by the cat and trying to pet the dog." She seems satisfied and her voice drops as if finished with the page until her eyes move to the depiction of the dog on the right and she continues, "But she's trying to slip away."

Hallie is doing many noteworthy things to orchestrate meanings in this opening of *Breakfast for Jack*. She searches the pages, and moves generally from left to right. She chooses the image of the cat on the right side to begin, deciding that the cat is climbing up on the person. However, she pauses and rereads changing her first reading, self-correcting to focus on the person who is trying to pet the dog as the cat rubs up against his legs. This is an important self-correction because it places the human character at the center of the action and allows Hallie to put that person in relation to the other characters: "Somebody's by the cat and trying to pet the dog." Once she has done this, her gaze lands again on the dog, who appears lively and perhaps about to leap up, and she reads, "But she's trying to slip away." Hallie's meaning-making move in which she puts the human being in the center of the action, leads her to then attend to and voice the intention of the dog in response: "But she's trying to slip away." Hallie adds this narration as she listens to her unfolding story.

Hallie has orchestrated meanings across three central images on the page—the cat, dog and person. At first the image of the cat seems to have salience for Hallie, perhaps because it is on the left side of the page and she is primarily looking left to right, or perhaps because the cat appears active, rubbing up against a person's leg. However, Hallie's self-correction suggests that the image of the person takes on salience during her sense-making as she seems to make sense of the pets as being in relation to the person, as she then narrates. This is particularly significant because the image of the person is incomplete, with only feet, legs, lower torso, and an arm showing, making it more ambiguous and difficult to transmediate.

Hallie continues to read with a predominately left to right gaze. However, the direction of her gaze does not always match her narration. Rather, Hallie searches left to right and then chooses salient images to narrate. For example, on the second page the boy on the right is putting on his bathrobe, while the cat and dog are on the left. The dog is quietly sitting on the floor watching the boy, while the cat is on the counter, crouched and looking at the boy with a wide-open mouth as if meowing loudly. Cans of pet food are beside the cat. Hallie reads, "And the kitty's up there," choosing the cat as the focus of her narration perhaps because the cat appears to be calling out to the boy, which increases Hallie's sense of being "addressed" by this vocalizing image.

On the next page of *Breakfast for Jack* Hallie rereads and self-corrects again. Here the boy is putting a dish of food down for the cat (whose mouth is still wide open) while the dog watches, looking a bit dejected. Hallie reads, "Him was giving the kitty . . . Jack was giving the cat food and the dog food." Hallie rereads and self-corrects to give the boy a name, changing the pronoun "him" to "Jack." While technically this is an inaccurate designation since Jack is the dog, Hallie has imagined that Jack is the boy—Jack is, after all, a boy's name. Hallie also looks back at the left side of the page at the dog (who is actually not being fed) as if to reconsider her reading, but instead turns the page. What is important in thinking about what Hallie is doing as a reader here is that she is correcting her own reading in light of the meanings she is constructing along the way; she is orchestrating meanings over narrative time as part of comprehending—something all good readers do.

In addition to choosing salient images to transmediate, rereading, and self-correcting her narration as she listens and responds to her own meaning-making, Hallie uses repetition and hesitation with the placeholder "*um*" to gain time for meaning-making. Toward the end of *Breakfast for Jack* the family is outside the house, going off in different directions; the boy is in the center of the page looking down at the ground as if something is wrong and, of course, Jack is still in the house unfed. Hallie reads, "And then . . . he . . . he . . . got off that . . . um . . . um . . . and he went home." In this utterance Hallie appears to be trying to figure out the image. Her eyes and her fingers

Table 2.1. Examples of Orchestration in Hallie's Reading of *Breakfast for Jack*

Searches/ chooses	Searches pages and chooses meanings	Gaze moves left to right and right to left on pages several times.
Pauses/ hesitates	Allows time to elapse before narrating	Uses "um"
Cross-checks/ selfcorrects	Checks images against her own narration	The kitty is climbing up . . . Somebody's by the cat trying to pet the dog.
Rereads/ self-corrects	Repeats words or phrases of narration	Him giving the kitty . . . Jack was giving the cat food and the dog food.

scan the page as she reads, hesitates, and finally ends this part of the reading with "and he went home" as she looks at and points to the closed front door of the house.

What does Hallie's reading of *Breakfast for Jack* tell us about the way she orchestrates across modes as part of comprehending? First, Hallie demonstrates a range of orchestrating activity. She searches, cross-checks, rereads, self-corrects, and uses pauses as she orchestrates between image, thought, and language (see Table 2.1). Hallie selects images carefully and omits many in her narration, choosing and transmediating in such a way as to create a meaningful narrative. Hallie's selection of images seems to reflect listening to her own meaning-making, and cross-checking meanings as she transmediates images into narration, rereads, and self-corrects.

Hallie effectively manages her dialogic engagement with the multiple meanings of *Breakfast for Jack*. As a dialogic object, *Breakfast for Jack* represents multiple subjectivities, often hinting at their interaction. Hallie meets and enacts these subjectivities using social imagination to voice characters' intentions—"and the dog's trying to get up there"—and feelings—"he's sad." As noted in Chapter 1, *Breakfast for Jack* is a text with multiple representations of time, changes in setting, and other qualities that challenge a reader's dialogic engagement with and within this storied world. Hallie successfully mediates this complexity for herself through searching and choosing, rereading, and self-correcting.

Responding to Hallie

Examining Hallie's reading gives us insight into the ways in which she orchestrates meanings with images and enacts those meanings in spoken narration. Hallie has demonstrated many strengths that can be the focus of a reading conversation. Remembering that Hallie is only 3 years old and somewhat shy, I might begin with,

Thank you, Hallie, for reading *Breakfast for Jack*. That was a fun book, wasn't it? Would you like to show me a place in the story you really liked?

By asking Hallie if she'd like to show me something about the story first, I can accomplish two aims of a reading conversation. First, I affirm for Hallie that this reading is hers and that as the reader she has important things to say about the story. Second, I learn more about her sense-making; what she chooses will likely be something that has importance to her. If possible I would use the place in the story she chooses to continue our conversation about her orchestration activity. If not, I might continue by saying,

I noticed some interesting things about your reading that I'd love to tell you about. How does that sound?

Having set up the conversation as one in which she will hear me think with her about her reading, I would first note how she chooses certain images rather than attempting to narrate them all:

You know, Hallie, when you were reading, I could see you looking at the pages carefully, like you were really paying attention to the pictures and figuring out the story. Sometimes you used a lot of the picture in your story and sometimes you decided to leave part of the picture out so it would make sense with your story. All good readers choose what to pay attention to. Let's look at a page where you did that.

In returning to parts of the story where Hallie omitted images, my primary purpose is to affirm that she is doing what all good readers do—choosing what meanings to attend to. But I am also interested in helping Hallie expand her sense-making to orchestrate the transmediation of more images.

On this page where the boy is getting his bathrobe on and the pets are waiting to be fed, you read "and the kitty's up there." Can you tell me about that?

Hallie's use of rereading and self-correcting are also a strength and one that will serve her well as a reader of both wordless books and books with print, a good point for a reading conversation.

Hallie, I really noticed you changing your mind during your reading. You would start reading one way and then look at the page again, and read it a different way. Changing your mind when you read because you are noticing and figuring out new things is an important thing to do in reading. Let me show you a place where you changed your mind.

Thinking with Hallie about her self-correcting emphasizes the importance of this kind of flexibility in reading. Notice that I would not likely use the term "self-correcting" with Hallie. Because of her age, it would probably not be a useful phrase for her at this point in her reading development, and it could be misunderstood as a need to correct her reading. If I were Hallie's teacher, I would be sure that Hallie continues to have books that challenge her with multiple varied meanings. I would end our conversation by offering Hallie a book to take with her for later reading, affirming her as a reader.

In outlining a possible reading conversation with Hallie, I have suggested several possibilities for actively discussing her comprehending activity in terms of orchestration. However, I would be sensitive to Hallie's young age and capacity for engaging in conversations about her reading. After all, reading *Breakfast for Jack* is now over, and she might be quite ready to move on to the other interesting things that await her in the rest of her preschool day. Reading conversations should always nurture love for books and for reading, and not create negativity around a child's relationships with books or around reading with her teacher.

Chloe's Orchestration Across Modes

We turn now to 6-year-old Chloe. Chloe's orchestration of images and resulting comprehending activity differ quite a bit from Hallie's. Though also quiet and serious, Chloe readily chimes in with me to read the title page, *I Had Measles*, but by inserting the word *Weasels* for *Measles,* she effectively takes over the reading from me right away! Chloe's agentive dialogue with the text begins immediately.

Like Hallie, Chloe searches the images across pages. However, Chloe has a more studied approach, as if mining them to use in her own evolving story. For example, on the first page spread—where the sick child is sleeping, the eager puppy is climbing up on her, and the brother is apparently trying to wake her—Chloe's gaze moves left to right. The sick child is larger and foregrounded, making her the salient character. The visual salience of this character, in addition to the first-person title, may guide Chloe's decision to make her own reading a first-person account. She begins by enacting the sick child and reading, "My dog won't leave me alone while I'm sleeping. I'm sick."

Consider what is involved in this initial, studied and decisive, first-person narration. This is an image of three characters: a child lying down, apparently sick; an eager, younger child leaning in on the sick one, trying to get her up; and a lively puppy. Reading these images means figuring out which one of the characters is sick (since we know that the story is about someone who has the measles) and what each character is up to—what they are thinking, feeling, and doing. Chloe does much of this in her opening of

"My dog won't leave me alone while I'm sleeping. I'm sick." She has decided who is sick, what the puppy is doing, and how the sick child is feeling (sick and a little annoyed at the puppy). As noted earlier, Hallie sidesteps these aspects of comprehending by limiting herself to a single character. Chloe, on the other hand, voices the sick child as the main character and orchestrates the meanings of the other images in relation to this character, whom she has become.

On the next page the image on the left shows the sick girl lifting her shirt while a female character, likely the mother, puts her hand on the child's spotted belly. Once again, the girl is larger and most of her body is in the illustration, which gives her salience. On the right, the sick child is foregrounded and sleeping in her bed. The mother, younger sibling, and puppy are apparently leaving the room. As Chloe views the two-page spread, her eyes move left to right and her gaze lands on the sleeping child. Chloe reads, "Get off me, dog, I have weasels." Chloe has ignored the left-hand image, where the puppy is not depicted, in favor of the right-hand image, which represents both the puppy and the sick child. Chloe's choosing activity mediates what she apprehends from the images—the dog leaving the room— with the evolving dialogue with and within this storied world of the main character. Her narration of "Get off me, dog" enacts the past according to the text—the boy is now at the door and not leaning over the child, trying to get her up—while keeping with the present tense of narrative time in her own story. Chloe orchestrates meanings across two narrative times: the narrative time represented in the text images and the narrative time unfolding in her own sense-making. To do this, she transmediates images as they occur in the sequence of the book, but ignores some (the whole left-hand image) and reorders others. She adjusts the verb tenses as necessary to enact meanings that flow within the narrative time of her own story. Chloe also uses narrative imagination to create new narrative elements in response to both the images and her own unfolding story. She actively cross-checks the images and her own meaning-making as she goes, instead of trying to match what she is narrating to the pictures. Chloe is a participant in this storied world and an active agent in her dialogue with this text.

Chloe continues her orchestration of images later in the reading. The left side of a page spread shows the sick child sitting up in bed and drinking an orange drink through a straw. On the right page, the sick child is in the background, asleep in her bed, while the younger child is squatting just outside the bedroom door, holding back an eager-looking puppy. Chloe looks left to right and then reads, "I will drink my juice. I will go back to bed. No one will mess with me." Her reading of the left -side page is straightforward and in the future tense. By reading, "I will go back to bed," Chloe explains what needs to happen in order for the right-hand illustration to make sense (the sick child is asleep and no longer drinking juice) and maintains her first-person, present tense account in the voice of the sick child. Finally, her last sentence for this page spread, "No one will mess with me," considers the foregrounded illustration of the younger child and puppy outside of the half-closed door, interprets it as leaving the sick child alone, and then orchestrates that understanding with her ongoing oral narrative. Her inflection and use of the phrase "mess with me" sustains her characterization of the sick child as not feeling well and being slightly annoyed with the puppy, and keeps her first person focus despite the foregrounding and resulting salience of the younger child and puppy outside the door.

Chloe orchestrates meanings from images in ways that help her sustain her first person focus again on the next page, where the mother is entering the room. In this image the mother appears actively coming towards the sick child with her arms out to the side and legs positioned as if walking. The image of the mother nearly fills the right side of the page. Both the implied action and the size of the mother's image give it salience. Yet Chloe stays with her first person account reading, "Whenever my mommy wakes me up, I wake up," mentioning, but not elaborating the character of the mother. To sum up Chloe's reading of *I Had Measles*, we see that she embarks on a first-person account, rather than positioning herself as an outside narrator. This positioning guides Chloe's orchestration across modes; that is, "being" the character of the sick child influences her decision-making about what to attend to and how to make sense of the images she encounters. At times, it is as if Chloe-as-the-sick-child is doing the reading. Her reading is inventive and takes on a life of its own as she moves through the story as first-person narrator. As she apprehends images and uses transmediation to render them in oral language, the coherence of her emerging narrative appears to guide how this transmediation occurs. She cross-checks what she sees in images with what is going on in her story, and ignores or reframes their potential meanings so they work with her own sense-making (see Table 2.2).

Responding to Chloe. These observations of Chloe's reading provide numerous talking points for a reading conversation. Chloe displays an active stance, sense of agency, and confidence in her ability to make meaning of this text. This sense of agency will serve Chloe well as she develops as a reader. It is a strength to notice and build on. After thanking Chloe for the reading and asking her if there is a part of the story she'd like to show me or talk about, I would acknowledge Chloe's decision-making by returning to specific pages of the text and commenting on her ownership of the story:

> Chloe, one thing I really liked about your reading was the way you made decisions about what to include and what was important to the story. All good readers choose what to pay attention to when they read. Let's look at a couple of those places.

Table 2.2. Examples of Orchestration in Chloe's Reading of *I Had Measles*

Searches/ chooses	Searches pages and chooses meanings	Gaze moves back and forth as if "mining" images.
		First-person choice shapes orchestration.
		Choosing involves enacting relationships.
		My dog won't leave me alone while I'm sleeping. I'm sick.
		Whenever my mommy wakes me up, I wake up.
Pauses/ hesitates	Allows time to pass before narrating	
Cross-checks	Checks images against her own narration	No one will mess with me.

Another important aspect of Chloe's reading is her way of becoming the main character and telling the story from that perspective. This is also an important part of print reading that can be shared with Chloe.

> Chloe, the first thing I noticed about your reading is that you told the story as if you were the girl that was sick. You invented things for her to say and imagined how she was feeling. Good readers often imagine the lives of characters. Can you tell me about that part of your reading? Let's go back and look at a couple of places where you did that.

Prompting Chloe to talk more about her focus on the character of the girl could also be a way to help her think more about the inner worlds of other characters.

> You know, Chloe, I noticed on one page you mention the mom who is waking up the sick girl, and on another you mention the dad outside. Let's look at one of those pages and think more about those characters. Would you like to choose? Good, here's the dad. You read, "I wish I can go to the playground with daddy, but I can't. I'm sick," really letting me know what the girl was thinking and feeling. I wonder what the dad might be thinking or feeling?

Asking Chloe to talk about other characters in an interested way might lead her to consider the multiple characters and their inner worlds and relationships, building on a strength already apparent in her reading.

As mentioned in the discussion of responding to Hallie's reading, there are also things to be cautious about in a reading conversation with Chloe.

For example, I would be careful to ascertain whether prompting her to think about other characters would feel like a "correction" to her reading of *I Had Measles*. The purpose of reading conversations is to enhance young children's experiences with wordless books. If stretching into other characters helps enhance Chloe's experience, then it suits the purpose. If asking her to consider other characters feels like a correction, it may detract rather than enlarge her reading experience. Being sensitive to how young children are actually experiencing reading and reading conversations is critical. Side-by-side reading as a relationally oriented context can support this needed sensitivity. Affirming Chloe's reading with a book suggestion, or one to take along with her, could end this reading conversation.

Maya's Orchestration Across Modes

Our third reader, Maya, was also 6 years old when she read *I Had Measles*. Maya has a serious stance toward this reading. She studies images and sometimes uses her fingers to point to them as she reads. Maya rarely looks up from the page, and gives the impression that she is engaged in her meaning-making. This engagement is also evident in her frequent searching of pages and scanning back and forth as she reads.

On the first double-page spread of *I Had Measles,* Maya looks back and forth across the page before she takes in the scene of the small boy trying to wake his older sister. Her eyes land on the left side of the page, where the sick girl is lying down underneath blankets. She starts her story with the pronoun "her" and then pauses, using "um" to gain some time. During this pause, Maya again looks back and forth across the pages and reads " . . . and her little brother is trying to wake her up." Based on this opening context, Maya may have intended to begin her story by choosing the sick girl on the left side of the page. Many of her utterances begin with "Her . . ." followed by some action related to the sick child. This would match how books work: They are read left to right. Her approach also matches the salience of the main character, who is foregrounded, larger, and in the vulnerable position of lying in bed on her side. In this way, the logic of the written language and image match.

But Maya changes her mind after scanning the images a second time. She reads, "and her little brother is trying to wake her up," and quickly adds, "and her crying, and her little dog's trying to wake her up too." Her decision to narrate the boy's action first may be a response to this image's addressivity. The illustration of the boy shows his arm raised over the covers, as if getting ready to pull them off his sister. His eyes are open and lips are slightly parted, as if he is speaking or getting ready to speak. This image of the animated boy and eager puppy captures Maya's attention and becomes the focus of her initial transmediation, rather than the more salient, larger, and foregrounded image of the sick girl. Maya chooses and narrates the action from right to left. It is also interesting to note that, unlike Chloe, Maya includes all the characters in her sense-making of this first page. She transmediates this image into multiple meanings and then orchestrates a set of relationships between characters that involve action and intention: The brother and the dog are *trying* to wake her up.

Maya seems to respond again to the particular addressivities of images later in the story. There is a page spread where the sick child is in bed on the left side and a woman wearing a stethoscope (apparently a doctor) is leaning over her, while another woman (apparently the mother) is opening curtains on the other side of the room. The child has a thermometer in her mouth. The right-side image depicts a man (apparently the father) foregrounded with his face fully visible. His one arm is outstretched, holding an orange drink. His other arm is carrying toys. Maya's eyes search both pages of these distinct images, which are ambiguous in terms of their relation to one another and within narrative time.

Maya scans back and forth across both sides of the page. She reads, "Him bringing her some—her bring, um, him bringing her some . . ." She begins with the character on the right and reads, "him bringing her some," but quickly changes this to "her bring" as she scans to the left, gazing at the image of the two women taking care of the sick child. Maya may have been trying to orchestrate meanings from the left-hand image by shifting her pronoun use to reflect the female characters. She cross-checks this choice with her dialogic enactment of this text and finds that it doesn't make sense with the action which she has chosen to narrate. She buys time using "um" and glances to the right again, where the man is standing, and proceeds with her reading: "him bringing her some iced tea." Like Chloe, Maya omits most of an image in service of her own ongoing sense-making. Referring only to the sick child ("her") and omitting the women via self-correction, she reads, "him bringing her some iced tea." This is an interesting example of how Maya transmediates meanings by orchestrating image-reading strategies to create a well-sequenced, meaningful narrative (see Table 2.3).

Maya also uses rereading to orchestrate meanings during this wordless book reading. Rereading in wordless book reading takes the form of repeating. For example, on the page where the younger child is coloring a picture, she reads, "The little brother coloring and the dog's—the dog's trying to sniff it." Maya repeats the short phrase "the dog's" as if using the repetition to gain some time to figure out what the dog is doing. She then returns to a phrase that she used earlier in the reading and reads, "the dog was sniffing the ground when the little boy, the dad, and the dog were out playing on the swings." Maya's rereading allows her time to orchestrate the meanings she is presently constructing with the rest of her narrative.

Maya, like Chloe, searches and cross-checks as she orchestrates meanings across modes while reading. Like Hallie, Maya pauses in order to think. Maya's orchestrating strategies include rereading and self-correcting. She

Table 2.3. Examples of Orchestration in Maya's Reading of *I Had Measles*

Searches/chooses	Searches pages and chooses meanings	Gaze moves left to right and right to left on pages several times.
Pauses/hesitates	Allows time to elapse before narrating	Uses "um" several times.
Cross-checks	Checks images against her own	Him bringing her some—her bring, um, him bringing her some iced tea.
Rereads/repeats	Repeats words or phrases of narration	Her, um, her little . . .
Self-corrects	Changes narration (word or phrase)	Her get—her got polka dots all over her. Him bringing her some—her bring, um, him bringing her some iced tea.

has a consistent linguistic pattern of using "Her" as the subject of all but her final sentence.

Responding to Maya. Maya's reading demonstrates several ways in which she orchestrates meanings and are strengths of her reading that can be built upon in a reading conversation. As with Hallie, I might address her flexibility as a reader and her willingness to change her mind. A reading conversation with Maya might begin something like this:

> Maya, when you were reading I noticed how much you studied the images and even changed your mind about how the story should go as you read. Let's look at a few places where you did this. Good readers do this all the time. We call it "self-correcting." Isn't that a funny way to say it? It just means that as readers read, they are always checking to make sure that what they are reading makes sense.

In this possible conversation, I use terminology I might not use with younger readers. At age 6 and in kindergarten, Maya is probably ready and able to apply specific language to how she thinks about her own reading, as her metacognitive abilities are likely developed enough for this to be meaningful.

A related point that could be addressed is Maya's hesitations and pauses, which she seems to use to gain time to think. Again, pausing to think is a useful orchestrating strategy for all kinds of reading that contributes to deep comprehension. Noticing this with Maya teaches her to value what she is already doing as a reader of wordless books.

> Maya, I noticed a couple of places where you seemed to pause as if you were thinking. You would say "um . . ." and wait a bit. I do that too when I am thinking about what to say. Pausing can be helpful when we read. Let me show you where in the story I heard you do this. Maybe you can tell me more about what you were thinking.

Inviting Maya to talk about her thinking at different places in the reading is asking her to do complicated work. She would not only have to go back to the story, but back to parts of her thinking that might not have been clear, places where she paused, hesitated, where she was unsure in her sense-making. This, then, would be a place to be cautious and sensitive to any sense of uncertainty Maya might be feeling. Being genuinely interested in children's comprehending and listening carefully to how they are experiencing this time with you is critical to the success of a reading conversation. As always, I would be sure to end the conversation with an affirmation of Maya and her reading by offering her a book or suggesting a book title as she moves into the rest of her day.

WHAT ORCHESTRATION CONTRIBUTES TO COMPREHENDING

Hallie, Chloe, and Maya have each demonstrated transmediation and the orchestration of meanings across modes. They enact this comprehending activity by apprehending images and responding to their addressivity, searching images, making choices about what to attend to, generating meanings from images, and transmediating those images into an ongoing oral narrative. Each reader also exerts her own sense of agency and works at her own level of complexity, demonstrating varying layers of richness and degrees of dialogic engagement.

In all three of these readings, characters and events are left behind as these young readers make choices, and the meanings they generate unfold, creating narratives of I Had Measles and Breakfast for Jack that hang together in a way that has its own logic. Though Hallie is only 3, she demonstrates orchestration during her reading of Breakfast for Jack that is similar to that of Chloe's and Maya's readings of I Had Measles.

The ability to orchestrate a set of coherent meanings from a range of potential meanings during reading is critical to the deep comprehending of any text. Apprehending and responding to addressivity—followed by searching, choosing, cross-checking, rereading, and self-correcting—are ways in which readers make meaning of printed texts (Clay, 1991; Goodman et al., 1987). While working with images instead of print, Hallie, Chloe, and Maya engaged in these kinds of comprehending activities in their own ways and to varying degrees of complexity as they engaged in the larger, generative, and inventive work of transmediating images during wordless book reading.

This inventive work involves not only moving across modes, but imagining and orchestrating synergistic relationships between text and image usually done by the authors and illustrators of picture books (Sipe, 1998). Children's capacities for creating relationships between image and story that "interanimate each other" (Meek, 1988) require imaginative engagement in the story world as part of the comprehending activity, and should not be overlooked as important to their personal sense-making and ongoing reading development.

We have also learned from Hallie, Chloe, and Maya that inventive orchestration during wordless book reading requires risk taking, as young readers navigate the ambiguities of story represented in image. Although wordless books are perhaps more obviously ambiguous than print texts, when readers transact with any narrative text they encounter storied worlds defined by layered, multiple, and sometimes ambiguous meanings that represent and reflect aspects of human experience. Paying attention to orchestration values the complexity of what young readers do as they take risks and try out, play with, and imagine possible meanings during reading—refining, rejecting, and affirming particular meanings as they go. Paying attention upholds their active processes, and diminishes the importance of getting reading "right." The orchestration activities of children's early comprehending made visible through wordless book reading are not accounted for in most assessments of emergent reading skills, which are so often designed to capture print-related skills or evaluate children's abilities to gain predetermined literal meanings. In this chapter we have seen how three young children engaged in active orchestration of meanings across the modes of the wordless book context as part of comprehending. This intricate orchestration of meanings can be noticed, valued, and talked about with young readers as a means of nurturing these important aspects of comprehending—ones they will need throughout their reading lives.

CHAPTER 3

Comprehending as Embodied

In the previous chapter we examined how children orchestrate meanings as they transmediate the images of wordless books into spoken narratives. An important aspect of this sense-making is becoming present to and active within story worlds. In this chapter I highlight the embodied nature of comprehending activity as children make themselves present to and active within story worlds. We will meet three young readers of different ages—Emma, Molina, and Trevor—and observe their embodied activity during side-by-side wordless book reading.

SENSE-MAKING AS EMBODIED

Children participate in human interaction through and with language. In addition to spoken language, children use their bodies to participate in these everyday language events. They utilize gesture, gaze, and prosody to enact and express meanings of and for others and themselves. This embodied nature of human experience is fundamental to meaningful relationships and an indispensable quality of communication (Streeck & Jordan, 2009). As active agents in the world, we seek out relationship. We use our bodies and read each other's bodies in order to form connections with one another. We do not merely make sense *of* something or someone, but *with* something or someone in contexts of participatory sense-making (Fuchs & De Jaeger, 2009). Meaning is enacted as we participate in it.

As noted in Chapter 1, when children read, texts ask them to participate in sense-making with others, within vicarious social contexts. In these storied worlds, readers use text symbols and representations to relate to and make sense of a range of unknown fictional others, their relationships, and their experiences (Lysaker et al., 2011). This is a relatively new challenge for young children. Unlike older readers with more experience of the abstract nature of texts, young readers often turn to familiar physical modes of expression used in actual, everyday social contexts in order to comprehend. Physical modes—gesture, prosody, gaze, and dramatization—mediate the challenge of sense-making with text and help children literally "get in touch" with story worlds. In other words, young children use their bodies to respond as they are "being turned to" or addressed by the text (Bakhtin, 1986), enacting their unique subjectivities (Garte, 2016) in relation to what they perceive, thereby externalizing themselves within the context of story. Embodied activity brings children into physical relation with the material of texts by making them present to story worlds—a first move in sense-making. Such physical presence opens them to dialogical engagement with story as well as to the transformative possibilities made possible by the symbolic resources of text (Zittoun, 2016). This embodied enactment of meaning, what I refer to as *body reading*, is comprehending activity. Observing and considering young children's body reading can deepen and extend our understanding of their comprehending activity and guide responses that might nurture it.

BODY READING: MODES OF ENACTMENT

Young children's body reading involves multiple modes of enactment including gaze, prosody, facial expression, gesture, and dramatization, which they use to participate in sense-making during wordless book reading. Each of these modes has particular qualities that can make distinct contributions to meaning-making, and are often used synergistically by children to make sense of wordless texts.

Meaning-Making Modes

The embodied enactments of gaze, prosody, facial expression, gesture and dramatization are *meaning-making modes*, or ways of constructing, enacting, and communicating meaning (Kress, 2009). In addition to talk, these modes serve as resources for sense-making in children's social and physical worlds. Children's uses of multiple modes during play and writing have been the focus of significant scholarly explorations (Rowe, 2015; Wohlwend, 2009), while their use of multiple modalities during reading, although similarly important, is less often explored. Each mode, a distinct semiotic resource, has unique meaning potential based on its past use (van Leeuwen, 2005). As children enact meanings using different modes for different purposes, they construct their modal histories and their patterns of modal use, as well as gain familiarity with how these resources work for them. Noting young children's modal preferences and uses over time can be useful in understanding their emergent comprehending activity, much like observing and noting children's reading strategy use in print reading can inform interpretations of their reading processes. In my work reading with young children, I have observed the following modes in children's readings of wordless books, embodiments that seem critical to comprehending.

Gaze. It may seem unnecessary to talk about gaze as a means of embodiment during reading. However, gaze is more than seeing. Gaze is an action that influences what is perceived and interpreted in visual and spatial modes (Lancaster, 2001). Children use gaze to navigate the visual–spatial territory of book pages. The movement of their gaze demonstrates what features are of interest, as well as how they perceive and construct connections between visual features across the spatial landscape.

Prosody. *Prosody* refers to the patterns of stress and intonation in human utterances. People rely on prosody to gauge the moods, intentions, and other aspects of meaning in everyday social interactions that are not necessarily conveyed by words. In print reading, we often pay attention to the prosody readers demonstrate when concerned with reading fluency, which in part, by definition, has to do with patterns of intonation (Rasinski, Rikli, & Johnston, 2009). Children's patterns of intonation and their abilities to "read smoothly" or "sound like readers" are considered important aspects of becoming proficient readers. We return to this aspect of children's comprehending in Chapter 6. In this chapter, however, we begin our exploration of prosody as an embodied aspect of enacting meaning with texts, particularly in synergy with other meaning-making modes.

Facial Expression. Facial expression is an indispensable part of communicating and sharing meaning. Reading faces is a critical human activity (Baron-Cohen, 2001), and using the face to enact meaning is equally vital. As teachers and researchers, we do not often consider facial expression when observing reading, except perhaps as used during planned dramatizations. However, the use of facial expression during young children's wordless book readings is integral to comprehending and enacting subjectivities within storied worlds.

Gesture and Body Positioning. How we position our bodies and move our fingers, hands, and arms communicates a range of meanings to others (McNeill, 2005). In print reading, we do not often consider gesture, since proficient readers' outward expressions of textual meanings are rare, again with the exception of planned dramatizations like Readers Theatre. However, young children use gesture and body positioning to spontaneously enact meanings during reading. Deictic gestures, like pointing and sweeping, in which children use their index fingers are especially apparent in young children's readings, and have been observed as important aspects of their writing (Rowe, 2015). Deictic gestures are critical to infant/toddler communication (Tomasello, Carpenter, & Liszkowski, 2007) and thus represent a mode of communication that has potent history for young children. These modal histories contribute to the meaning potential of these gestures for young children as they interact with books.

Dramatization. I use the word *dramatization* to refer to children's overt dramatic enactment of meanings as they occur during reading. In classrooms with young children, dramatization happens spontaneously. With older children, dramatization may occur as part of Readers Theatre (Worthy & Broaddus, 2001/2002). Dramatization is valued as a way to develop reading fluency and build comprehension. In wordless book reading, young children use dramatization as a means of spontaneously enacting and communicating meanings in conjunction with spoken narrations, or when their spoken narrations fall short of the meanings they want to enact.

Modal Intensity, Complexity, and Density

While describing each mode as distinct helps highlight their particular qualities as semiotic resourses, most often multiple modes are used synergistically in meaning-making interactions (Jewitt, 2009), including the interaction of children and texts during wordless book reading. For example, while children inevitably use gaze to take in the images on the pages, they may also use pointing to follow meaning, or dramatization to enact those meanings. How modes are used together to make meaning gives us information about children's body readings and the particular ways in which they use their bodies to make sense of text. To gauge the relative importance of modes in an interaction, in this case the interaction of child and text, we can note the intensity, complexity, and density of modal use (Norris, 2004). *Modal intensity* refers to "the weight or importance of a specific mode." As Norris (2004) describes it, if a mode has intensity in a particular interaction, that interaction could not happen the same way without it—meaning-making hinges on it. Children's modal use during reading, as another kind of human interaction, can also be defined by modal intensities. For example, a child's use of pointing to follow and lead their narration or their use of facial expression to enact characters' thoughts and feelings can "make" the reading. Modal complexity is also important to understanding the meaning-making that constitutes any interaction. An interaction has *modal complexity* when modes are, as Norris (2004) puts it, "intricately intertwined" (p. 79). Children demonstrate modal complexity during reading with their concurrent, synchronized use of multiple modes to enact meaning; for example, the use of prosody simultaneous with facial expression in comprehending characters. Lastly, *modal density* refers to the combined modal weight accomplished by the use of one or more highly intense modes, or the less intense use of several modes. Modal density is arrived at through modal intensity, complexity, or their combination (Norris, 2004). Noting these qualities of modal use can be useful in making sense of children's embodied comprehending because they represent children's preferences for modal use during reading and bring their active comprehending to light.

EMMA, MOLINA, AND TREVOR

Emma, Molina, and Trevor all attended the Head Start preschool. Emma is White and was barely 3 years old; Molina is also White and was 4 years old; and Trevor is Black and was just over 5 years old when they read with me at the Reading Table outside their classrooms. Emma, Molina, and Trevor provide illustrative demonstrations of embodied comprehending during their wordless book readings. Noting children's use of their bodies and their particular modal choices allows us to affirm and enhance these important ways young children make sense of narrative worlds. Full verbal transcripts of their wordless book readings can be found in the online resources for this chapter (see online Appendixes 3.A, 3.B, and 3.C at www.tcpress.com).

Emma's Body Reading of *Breakfast for Jack*

Let's begin with Emma's reading of *Breakfast for Jack*. Emma chooses this particular wordless book from the collection at the Reading Table, picking it up quickly before she settles in her chair. Emma appears eager to read *Breakfast for Jack* with me, and looks to me as she says, "I read this first, then that," pointing to another book on the table.

Opening *Breakfast for Jack*, Emma stops and points at the end papers, where numerous cans of dog food cover the pages. She points to one of the cans on the left-hand page, looks up at me with a laughing smile and says, "There's cans," as if it is quite silly to see cans on the inside cover of the book. Emma then quickly turns the pages, inadvertently turning more than one. She reads, "The last day the dog was . . . " immediately focusing on the main character. In an effort to capture her whole reading, I interrupt her and turn back the pages so she can start at the beginning. She begins again and her gaze follows her fingers as she immediately points to the cat on the left-hand side of the page and reads, "The cat was on the people. That he was sleeping. Then he couldn't go to awake because he was sleepin'." She then looks up at me, as if to be sure I understand, rather than to gain my affirmation. This pattern of pointing to the images with gaze in tandem and then looking up at me is something Emma does throughout her reading of *Breakfast for Jack*. Emma's gaze moves most often, but not exclusively, from left to right. She is both present to the book and to me, actively enacting her subjectivity in both actual and vicarious social contexts. In fact, the liveliness of her subjectivity, which is enacted through gaze and pointing, has modal intensity and complexity. Her reading wouldn't be the same without the synergistic use of these modes. Emma's predilection to be present and seek intersubjective connection makes reading with her a delightful experience.

In addition to using pointing at nearly every page turn, Emma often uses facial expression in her reading of *Breakfast for Jack*. As she enacts

Table 3.1. Examples of Modal Use in Emma's Body Reading of *Breakfast for Jack*

Gaze/ pointing	Enacting subjectivity/locating self in storied world	Points to characters as she narrates
	Sharing meanings with me	Looks at me after narrating
Dramatization	Enacting word meanings	Makes the motion of opening a can for the word *can opener*
Facial expression and prosody	Enacting characters' thoughts and feelings	Shows sadness for dog being left alone

the characters' emotions with her face, she also expresses that emotion with her voice. For example, when the cat is fed first and the dog appears to be ignored, Emma reads, "He was sad," making a sad face as her voice drops in pitch. Emma uses her body to enact characters and bring them to life. Toward the end of the story, when the family leaves without feeding the dog, Emma reads, "Wait a minute, don't leave without *me*," voicing a sad and imploring Jack. She turns to me and adds, with a somber expression, "And they're leaving without him. By his self," as if making sure that I understand just how awful this situation is.

In addition to using pointing, facial expression, and voice inflection, Emma uses dramatization as a comprehending activity. On one page of *Breakfast for Jack*, the boy is opening a can of food for the cat. Emma reads, "Then he was (inaudible) the . . . turning . . . turning the can," and makes the motion of opening a can with a can opener while looking at me as part of her explanation. She uses her body to work out word meanings in support of her narrative.

Emma uses her body throughout her reading of *Breakfast for Jack* through deictic gesture, facial expression, prosody, and even dramatization (see Table 3.1). Pointing with gaze and facial expression produce the greatest modal intensity and the reading as a whole has modal complexity as Emma synchronizes modes throughout the reading in service of meaning. Emma finishes *Breakfast for Jack* with the same energetic decisiveness with which she began, gets up, pushes in her chair, as she tells me she doesn't want to read another one, and goes back happily to her classroom.

Responding to Emma

Emma enacted her presence to the world of the story and her engagement in sense-making as a reader, and her engagement in the world of the story, with multiple synergistically related modes. Pointing, facial expression, prosody, and dramatization all helped Emma in comprehending *Breakfast for Jack*. Her energetic body reading was also fast paced. Noting these aspects of her reading, how might a reading conversation with Emma go?

Because of her level of activity and her young age, I would not necessarily try to engage Emma immediately in a reflective conversation about her reading. Requiring her to revisit this text would be artificial and unrelated to her lively interest in the next classroom activity, and as such would not contribute to authentic insights into her comprehending. Rather, I would find another opportunity to read *Breakfast for Jack* with Emma and re-create a context for the exploration of her comprehending activity.

> Emma, do you know what I noticed when you were reading *Breakfast for Jack*? You really used your hands, especially your fingers, to help you. Let me show you where I noticed you used your hands to make sense of the story.
>
> One way you used your fingers was to point. You pointed to places on the pages, sometimes before you even started reading. Finding your reading place is an important thing to do when you read any book, and your fingers really helped you.
>
> You know, Emma, I noticed that another way you used your fingers when you were reading was to point to yourself and to me. You did this when you were naming the characters. You used your hands to show that you were thinking about how our names could become the characters names. Do you remember? Your fingers seemed to get your thinking going about the characters and what their names might be. That's just what really good readers do. They are always making connections between their real lives and the lives of characters in stories.

During her first reading of *Breakfast for Jack*, Emma enacted the feelings of the dog and showed personal involvement in his predicament. Her use of facial expression and prosody to enact the sadness of the dog, for example, demonstrated her ability to think about the thoughts and feelings of characters. In her reading, however, she didn't attend to the feelings of any other characters. This could become a focus of reading conversation. While revisiting the book, I might respond to this aspect of her body reading by noticing her use of synchronous multiple modes to enact feelings and bring characters to life:

> Emma, one of my favorite parts of your reading was on the page where the dog Jack and the boy are looking at each other while the boy is eating breakfast. Jack's mouth is open, like he might be barking. When you read this page you made your face look so sad, just like what you imagined Jack was feeling. Then you read, "He was sad." When you made a sad face, you also made your voice sound sad just like you were imagining the character.

> I could tell you were really feeling how he must have been feeling. And then you looked at the boy on the page and read, "Oh dog, what are you doing?" You were imagining what the boy was thinking and saying to Jack. You did such a good job really being the characters. All good readers imagine what characters are thinking and feeling when they read.

After engaging Emma in a conversation about her reading of this page I might then prompt her to consider other characters on other pages, if she doesn't mention them herself. For example, at the end of the book where the family is on their way out the front door with Jack looking on and the cat sleeping, Emma again focuses solely on the dog. I might say,

> Let's look at this page at the end of the story, Emma. You were so upset that the family was leaving Jack alone. You even imagined what Jack might have been saying. You read, "Wait a minute, don't leave without me!" That was such good reading you did. I wonder if you can imagine what the mother, father, or children are saying as they leave the house?

In this way, I am purposefully working with Emma to expand a strength she has already demonstrated and see if, with conversation, she can broaden her navigation of this landscape of consciousness to include other characters. I may also discover that she was already imagining these aspects of the story, but because of her fast pace simply didn't include them. As a teacher reading with Emma, this would be important information, since it demonstrates her understanding of characters.

However, interrupting Emma frequently during a reading would seem to work against, and in some ways disrespect, her active agentive approach to meaning-making with books. So rather than many verbalized questions, I might also simply point to characters as she reads to see if my noticing of characters in this way might inspire her to think more about their thoughts and feelings. Because of Emma's energetic first reading and delight in the characters, I would offer Emma another in the series, like *When Jack Goes Out* (Schories, 2010).

Molina's Body Reading of *Float*

Our next reader, Molina, was 4 years old when she read *Float* with me. Molina was familiar with *Float* from classroom reading experiences with her teacher and was eager to read it when she came to the Reading Table. Though I keep this in mind, as important contextual information, I am interested in seeing what Molina does to comprehend this text as an independent meaning-maker.

As Molina begins, her immediate focus is the main character. She flips quickly through the end papers and title pages until she comes to an image of the main character. A moment before beginning to narrate, her gaze lands on the right side of the page and she points to the boy. She reads, "The little girl . . . the little girl went to make that paper just like a boat and . . . " Molina uses pointing in conjunction with gaze to connect herself to the story as narrator. Like Emma's pointing to the character, physically touching him with her index finger allows Molina to enter the storied world and locate herself as narrator in a particular narrative place and time. Pointing initiates her dialogic transaction with this text and enacts her subjectivity in response to the images. She means with her hands. Her subjectivity is further reflected in her narration. She calls the main character a little girl (a person of her own gender), a decision that reflects her presence and dialogic engagement with the storied world.

Molina also uses her body to enact her understanding of the main character during her reading of *Float*. On the second full page of *Float*, where the young child appears to be excited by the first drop of rain hitting her hand, Molina first points to the child on the right, saying, "the little girl." She continues, "and the little girl, the little girl does, the little girl does a little cry." As she works through this utterance, she simultaneously sweeps her index finger quickly up and down over the illustration of the character's face. The repetitive sweeping motion reflects the repetition of her spoken narrative and enacts her presence to the sadness of the girl in addition to Molina's own intense feelings as she imagines the character crying. She uses a sweeping gesture again when enacting the intense rainstorm depicted a bit later in the story. Molina strokes the child's face, which is barely visible in all the rain, as if expressing her own concern for the character who looks lost, and says, "Because her gone forever, because her right there in the rain." She uses gesture yet again to enact the intensity of the rain itself, moving her fingers up and down very quickly in a vertical motion over the lines of pouring rain represented in the image. Molina uses sweeping to enact and emphasize the meaning density of both story action and character's thoughts and feelings.

For Molina, pointing is also closely synchronized with gaze. Molina's uses of pointing and gaze are nearly simultaneous, happening at either the same time or in quick succession. In the examples above, and on nearly every page, Molina's use of gaze in conjunction with her deictic gestures often include studying illustrations and leaning in with her body as if to get a better look at what is happening.

While deictic gestures (pointing and sweeping with the index fingers) have high intensity for Molina during this reading, she also uses prosody with facial expression to enact the feelings of the main character (see Table 3.2). Just after she sweeps across the character's face and reads, "And the little girl, the little girl does, the little girl does a little cry," she goes on to read, "Oh! And it's raining!" Here she speaks the phrases with an intonation of

Table 3.2. Examples of Modal Use in Molina's Body Reading of *Float*

Gaze/ pointing	Enacting subjectivity	Points on nearly every page
	Locating self in storied world	Pointing sometimes precedes narration and leads meaning
	Leading/following meaning	
		Pointing is highly synchronized with gaze
Sweeping	Emphasizing characters' feelings	Sweeps over the face of the character "lost" in the rain
Other gestures	Emphasizing aspects of story	Opening arms, It's a beautiful day!
Facial expression	Enacting characters' thoughts and feelings	Shows sadness for the little girl in the rain

surprise. As she says, "Oh!" she opens her eyes wide, draws in her breath, and moves her body away from the book slightly, as if she is shocked by the image of the character catching the first raindrop in his hand.

She then returns to the image of the character farthest to the right, who is trying to cover himself from the light rain. She reads in a soft voice with low tone, "Because her sad . . . " and slightly stretches out the word *sad*. Her voice rises and falls to make meanings come to life in sound. While she reads, her face shows the sadness of the little girl, her voice drops, and she directs her gaze at the character.

Molina uses her body to communicate and play with word meanings. At the end of *Float,* when the rainstorm is over and the sun comes out, the main character is running with his arms raised and a paper airplane in one hand, as if getting ready to throw it into the air. Molina uses the same gesture to enact the exuberance of this ending. When she reads, "And it's a beautiful day!" she opens her arms wide, as if to embrace the sunshine that engulfs the character in the final pages of the story. Molina's enactment of the beautiful day demonstrates an understanding that goes beyond her words. Her embodied response shows that she understands this as a wonderful moment, one that is now alive in her body as a feeling of joy that she herself may have once felt. Her enactment of "beautiful day" makes it a personally felt meaning, and one that demonstrates her dialogic engagement with the storied world.

Responding to Molina

Let's now use observations of Molina's reading to guide a reading conversation. First, as demonstrated in Chapter 2, a moment for authentic personal response is a good place to start:

> Thank you for reading to me today, Molina, I enjoyed the story you created.

Offering Molina a chance to choose a place in the book she'd like to return to would be a good next step. Then it is time to turn to a thoughtful comment about how she enacted meaning through her body, communicating to Molina that what she is doing is what good 4-year-old readers do. In Molina's case, her use of pointing and sweeping have the greatest intensity. I would notice this by simply saying:

> Molina, do you know what I noticed when you were reading *Float*? You really used your hands, especially your fingers, to help you read. You pointed to places on the pages before you read the story. Finding your reading place is an important thing to do when you read any book and your fingers really helped you. Let me show you where I noticed you used your hands to make sense of the story.

Noticing where in the book Molina used her hands, and revisiting those pages with her, brings Molina back to the world of story, where she can revisit her meaning-making. Although Molina used gestures and facial expressions less frequently than she did pointing, all of these modes were quite important to her meaning-making and contributed to its modal complexity. Gestures and facial expressions were synchronized with other modes, as well as with the overall density of her enactment of story. I would respond as follows:

> I could tell that you really felt how sad the little girl was by the expression you made with your face. *You* looked so sad. And the way you held your arms out when you read "it's a beautiful day" at the end showed me you knew how important that was for the little girl. Really understanding how characters feel about what is happening around them is something good readers do all the time, even grownups.

Revisiting *Float* with Molina through a brief conversation affirms her personal sense-making in concrete ways. These kinds of conversations encourage her active engagement in sense-making as well as the joy and importance of revisiting books with others. Toward that end, I might suggest to Molina that a friend might enjoy hearing her read *Float* and offer her a time to do just that.

Trevor's Body Reading of *Breakfast for Jack*

Let's now turn to Trevor's reading of *Breakfast for Jack* for further examples of young children's body reading. Trevor comes quietly to the Reading Table and chooses *Breakfast for Jack*, telling me that he had read it with his class.

Trevor is soft-spoken and cheerfully intent on the book, and looks up at me very briefly just once as I describe our side-by-side reading for the day. At 5 years old, Trevor is the oldest of the three readers in this chapter and, as we will see, his body reading is distinctly different from the younger children.

From the outset Trevor is focused on the book. In Trevor's reading, deictic gestures, pointing and sweeping, have the most modal intensity; they characterize his reading. Trevor points, or sweeps, nearly continually in his reading of *Breakfast for Jack*, pointing to or just above images once each page is turned. Unlike Emma and Molina, he never uses dramatization and his facial expression remains constant as he reads.

On the opening page, Trevor begins by running his hands back and forth across the pages reading, "First there's a kitty and a dog." Trevor is not pointing to anything specific. Rather it is as if his hands are surveying the page for important features, which leads him to labeling the characters. However, after this opening Trevor points to some specific aspect of the images on every page. His pointing appears to have at least two different functions. First, he uses pointing to link images to his own thinking—a physical transaction between reader and text, which then makes meanings available to him for his narration. For example, on the page where the boy is feeding the cat while Jack looks on, Trevor reads, "The cat was, the cat was . . . ." then he points to the cat and continues, "opening his mouth." Pointing appears to help Trevor know his own thoughts, which Goldin-Meadow (2003) argues is a primary function of gesture in young children's interactions with others. In this case, it is the interaction with text that pointing aids.

Later on, Trevor uses pointing to share meanings with me. His gesture guides me to see what he is seeing, and see with him. For example, on the page with multiple images of Jack, Trevor reads, "There's . . .," as part of the utterance, "There's a lot of dogs." Pointing to the dogs and labeling them using "There's" seems addressed to me: "See what I am seeing." Trevor is showing me something, showing me that he knows about it, and showing me that he wants me to know that he knows. Thus pointing establishes a brief moment of sharedness between Trevor, me, and the book. He may even be inviting me to think about these multiple images with him, which I can take up in a later reading conversation. Unlike Emma, who turns away from the book to make eye contact with me and to establish this shared experience, Trevor relies on pointing and maintains his gaze on the book. His text-focused stance reminds me of young beginning readers of print texts, who stay glued to the book because they are aware of their need to track words across the page. As a pre-K 5-year-old, Trevor may be developing this practice of attentiveness to text.

Another example of how Trevor uses deictic gesture as part of comprehending occurs on a page that presents particular challenges to young children. In this part of the story, the author indicates the passage of time by depicting Jack and the cat in a series of images in which the cat eats, walks away, and then leaves the room, with Jack staring at his empty bowl. On this

Table 3.3. Examples of Modal Use in Trevor's Body Reading of *Breakfast for Jack*

Gaze/ pointing	Locating self in the storied world	Points to some aspect of the illustration on most page spreads
	Enacting subjectivity	Synchronizes pointing with gaze
	Leading/following meaning	Sometimes precedes narration (leads meaning), and sometimes occurs with or slightly after narration (following meaning)
Sweeping	Explores relationships between images	Sweeps fingers back and forth between multiple images of Jack on the same page

page, instead of pointing to particular images on the page, Trevor sweeps his fingers up and down the page between the images of this time-layered series. He counts the number of dogs and cats, as he sweeps, tallying them as if they were meant to be different animals rather than the same animals represented over time. He then points multiple times within a few seconds as he moves around both pages continuing his effort to make sense of how many dogs and cats there are.

In fact, Trevor points to, or sweeps across, characters using his fingers to connect with characters on every page turn, except for the first page. His pointing guides his comprehending by locating him in the visual–spatial landscape of a narrator as he moves through the story and connects meaning across pages. Pointing reflects his enactment of subjectivity—his understanding of himself in relation to the text. Trevor uses gesture to connect to and know his thoughts (Goldin-Meadow, 2003) while his steady, intense gaze appears analytic (Lancaster, 2001) and serves as a critical resource for him as he interprets visual and symbolic representations. Pointing to representations of objects and people in illustrations indicates, tracks, and leads meaning-making during wordless book reading.

Both gaze and pointing are high intensity modes for Trevor and the co-occurrence of speech, gaze, and pointing constitute the modal density of his transaction with this text (see Table 3.3). The coordination of gaze and pointing is important to his sense-making of this wordless text, but also can be seen as important aspects of print reading as well. As Trevor begins his independent reading of print text, gaze and pointing will be used to guide the voice–print match necessary to successful beginning reading.

Responding to Trevor

Observing Trevor's body reading of *Breakfast for Jack* provides several places to begin a reading conversation. Of course, a chance for Trevor to choose a place to revisit can come first. Then an authentic and positive response to Trevor would be that I really noticed how focused he was during the reading and how much he seemed to enjoy it. As a teacher, I would be interested in confirming these aspects of his reading since focus and enjoyment are important to his development as a reader. I would then turn to his use of pointing and sweeping as a means of sense-making. As in my conversation with Molina, I might first comment on the use of pointing to help him find his place in the text and give him a focus for his narration. I might say something like this:

> Trevor, one thing I noticed about your reading is that you pointed to pictures on almost every page, and then you used those pictures in your reading. Your fingers helped you make your story of *Breakfast for Jack*. You know, when readers are starting to read books with words they use their fingers too. It helps them keep track of where they are on the page.

Beyond this general comment, I would address some specific places where his use of deictic gestures, both pointing and sweeping, were particularly important to his reading.

> You know, Trevor, on this page where the cat is being fed you seemed to hesitate a little. You read, "The cat was, the cat was . . .," as if you weren't quite sure, but then when you pointed to the cat you finished your thought by saying he was "opening his mouth." Pointing really seemed to help you know what you were thinking and trying to say. Sometimes pointing can really help readers focus on something in a book and connect it to their own thinking.

Because Trevor's reading is nearly exclusively about objects and actions, reflective of Bruner's (1986) "landscape of action," I might continue this reading conversation to see if I can help him extend his sense-making into the "landscape of consciousness" or the inner worlds of characters.

> Let's look again at this part of the story. You are so right that the cat is really opening his mouth right here where you pointed. And I see that the boy is putting down some cat food, and Jack is just watching. I wonder what you think the cat might be thinking or feeling as the boy feeds him, or maybe even what Jack might be thinking or feeling watching the cat get fed . . . and not him.

As I engaged in this conversation with Trevor, I would use pointing myself to move from character to character as a means of fostering joint attention and shared meanings, as Trevor did with me. As noted in earlier reading conversations, this kind of extension should maintain a positive caring tone so that Trevor feels the conversation as an invitation to reenter the story and further explore meanings, rather than as the correction of a flaw.

I would also revisit the part of the story where the author is using multiple images to create a time sequence. In doing this, I am taking the lead from Trevor. His active sweeping and pointing and inviting me to share in his meaning-making about how many dogs there were on these pages demonstrates interest and inquiry into this unusual set of images. As a teacher, I would want to help him pursue this inquiry.

> You know Trevor, I really want to go back to those pages where there were all those dogs. I remember you were using your hands to show me. You even seemed kind of surprised by how many dogs you saw. Let's take a look and see if we can figure out how many different dogs there are.

Trevor was so actively engaged in making sense of these two pages, I would expect him to accept my invitation to revisit these images. As we noticed the images together, I would guide him to think about whether the dogs all looked like Jack or if they looked like other dogs, and then talk with him about this special use of a series of images to show things happening one after another. In this way, I am using his body reading as an indicator of active sense-making and inquiry to which I could respond instructionally with information about the depiction of time in images. If Trevor responded to this conversation about the series of images, I would offer him *Jack and the Missing Piece* (2004), another Schories book that does something similar.

WHAT BODY READING CONTRIBUTES TO COMPREHENDING

Emma, Molina, and Trevor each demonstrate in their own ways that young children use their bodies to comprehend. Specific comprehending activities are evident in this careful examination of their body readings: (1) finding their place as readers by connecting to the story world through bodily enactment of subjectivity; (2) connecting to characters and bringing them to life; (3) leading and following meanings; (4) emphasizing meanings and their importance; and (5) playing with meanings of words and phrases. These aspects of comprehending are important regardless of the age of the reader or the sophistication of the text. Accordingly, these activities are critical as processes themselves, regardless of the narratives produced or what children might "take away" from the reading.

A careful look at Emma, Molina, and Trevor shows how they use their bodies to accomplish this comprehending work. All three readers use gaze in both searching and studied ways to apprehend the subjectivities expressed in the images of *Breakfast for Jack* and *Float*. Each reader also enacts subjectivity through pointing, making themselves present to storied worlds, and initiating a dialogue with the text. Deictic gestures like pointing have modal intensity for Molina and Trevor—their enactment of meaning depends on these gestures. Pointing also helps them lead and follow meaning with gaze and spoken narration as they navigate the visual–spatial landscape of wordless text. Pointing not only enacts meaning, but also aids what Bertau (2014) calls "willingness to follow," a necessary condition for meaningful language events of all kinds (p. 450). Pointing helps Molina and Trevor follow meanings as represented in the texts, forming and getting to know their own thoughts as they watch their own gestures move across the pages. Pointing is a concrete means of transacting with text. The reader's body connects to the story world as part of a creative and constructive enactment of meanings.

Although less modally intense, pointing is also used by all three readers to synchronize their gaze with their deictic gestures. While early readers use pointing to track print, in emergent reading, particularly the emergent reading of wordless books, pointing has a different role of locating particular meanings and bringing gaze to bear in the enactment of subjectivity. Children make eye contact with characters and "see" authors' meanings. The synchronized use of gaze and pointing affords a physical conduit to an abstract world.

Beyond gaze and pointing, Emma and Molina use facial expression and prosody to enact characters, particularly the somewhat hidden inner worlds of their thoughts and feelings. This ability to make sense of the "landscape of consciousness" represented in peopled, storied worlds is critical to comprehending any narrative, an ability they will depend on throughout their reading lives.

In addition to becoming present to storied worlds, leading and following meaning, and enacting characters, Emma, Molina, and Trevor all use their bodies to explore specific word meanings. Because children author the linguistic text during wordless book reading, wordless books are interesting spaces to play with vocabulary. The necessity of generating words to represent meanings sometimes presents a challenge. Body reading deepens children's comprehending as they use their bodies to express and enact specific meanings; for example, Emma's bodily depiction of the can opener.

These brief examples of children's body reading demonstrate the importance of the body in young children's comprehending. Emma, Molina, and Trevor use multiple body reading modes and synchronize them into personal assemblages of modal enactment in service of their comprehending activity. Noticing and responding to children's body reading is one way to value and nurture their personal meaning-making. While it is challenging in the busyness of classroom life to find time to read one-on-one with children, this simple act of being present and responsive to a child's sense-making is in itself powerful teaching—an idea I will return to in Chapter 7. Beyond being present, it is important to think about body reading conversations with young children as times for affirmation of what they already are doing to enact meaning, and not necessarily times for coaching these embodied

responses, as we might do with reading strategies. Much like the disap-
pearance of pointing to words and the emergence of reading "in the head,"
the externalized, embodied comprehending activities used by young readers
will, in time, give way to the subtler and internalized embodied responses of
older readers. This transition will most likely not require shaping by teachers.

Paying attention to body reading also decenters and diminishes the central role of verbal language usually given to understanding what children are
doing when they read. Often, traditional assessments of emergent reading,
including wordless book reading (Paris & Paris, 2003), rely heavily on the
spoken narratives children produce. While these narratives are important
(and will be the focus of other chapters in this book), attending to only
verbal language risks overvaluing a single meaning-making mode. This is
especially detrimental when assessing emergent reading. Emma, Molina,
and Trevor have taught us that very young children can engage in intense,
complex, and multimodal activity when making meaning with books.

Lastly, and perhaps most importantly, noticing the embodied responses
of young children during their wordless book reading lets them know that
their embodied enactments are valuable tools for sense-making with books.
As mentioned earlier, all people rely on their unique repertoire of modal
use to connect with and make sense of and with others. Talking with young
children about what we see them doing as they engage in making meaning
with books is one way to affirm and draw attention to their uniqueness as
young readers and as human beings. Being aware of the idea that children
are enacting subjectivity every time they read reminds us that we are in the
presence of developing human beings who are enacting meanings and selves
right before our eyes.

CHAPTER 4

Comprehending as Imaginative Relationship with Text

Response, Recognition, and Recontextualization

In this chapter we begin a two-chapter examination of the relational and imaginative activities of children's comprehending during wordless book reading as made evident in their narratives. I describe the specific aspects of this relational activity—response, recognition, and recontextualization—as ways in which children imaginatively enact the relationships of their comprehending. I necessarily uncouple response, recognition, and recontextualization from related aspects of comprehending as well as from each other. While this approach is somewhat artificial, making distinctions between these related processes can make them more apparent and more valued as human sense-making activities that young children engage in when comprehending. Response, recognition, and recontextualization are influenced by readers' emotions as well as the texts they are reading. However, while response may be intuitive, immediate, and more dependent upon emotion, recognition and recontextualization rely heavily on the imagination.

EMOTION AND IMAGINATION

Making sense of storied worlds necessarily involves leaving the "here and now" of the actual concrete present to enter the "there and then" of story. Readers partially let go of their present realities in order to reconstruct new meanings with narrative others during comprehending. Readers of all ages experience this otherworldliness of reading, and for many it is the appeal. Getting lost in a book can be a wonderful experience and part of a rewarding reading life.

However, "letting go" can be daunting, particularly for young children who may just be developing the trust necessary to allow themselves into the story world. Without early story experiences, like lap reading, in which caring adults provide a secure, shared context for children to fall safely into stories and explore with ease, letting go can be a new and difficult challenge for preschool children (Bus & Van Ijzendoorn, 1995). Madeline Grumet

(1988) reflects this idea in her essay "Body Reading," where she suggests that "reading is fraught with danger" (p. 136) because readers must leave some part of themselves behind to participate in unfamiliar storied worlds.

Emotional responses to texts, in this case responses to the addressivity of images (Bakhtin, 1981), can override the daunting task of letting go. As mentioned in Chapter 1, *addressivity*, or the quality of turning to someone, is more accessible to young children because of the particular affordances of image, which "turn to" them in the familiarity of line, shape, and color, rather than abstract linguistic code, more effectively inviting response. A child's emotional response can draw them into the narrative world and make that move worth the risk. Emotion, then, as it functions in children's initial responses to text, is the draw: a sensation that propels readers toward new experiences in the peopled narrative landscape. In this way, a reader's initial emotional response is a leading activity of comprehending (Leont'ev, 1981; Vygotsky, 1967) that provides the context in which "new psychological processes arise or old processes are reorganized into novel forms" (Duncan & Tarulli, 2010, p. 272). Emotion surrounds, permeates, and fuels the initial responses to text. Paying attention to children's initial emotional responses to texts can guide teachers in their selection of books for their young readers.

If emotion is what leads young readers to the edge of the narrative world, imagination lands them squarely within it. As described in Chapter 1, imagination is an integral part of the comprehending activity. Imagination expands experience so that readers can move beyond their concrete place and time into storied worlds. In recognition and recontextualization, imagination allows readers to see themselves in narrative worlds and resituate their experiences within them, where they form relationships with and within the text worlds. Imagination is the means by which relationality is accomplished during comprehending.

Role of Texts

Comprehending happens in relation to texts, and so texts matter. As mentioned in Chapter 1, narrative texts in particular can be rich dialogic objects, vicarious social contexts and participation genres in which readers meet and enact relationships with characters, the subjectivities represented in storied worlds. Readers are "addressed" by texts: texts "say something" to readers so that texts and readers can become "speaking–listening partners" (Bertau, 2007) *if* the readers respond. In narrative texts this addressivity involves invitations to the reader to form relationships with and within the narrative world. Addressivity and the invitations that are a part of a text's addressivity contribute to its *sense of hospitality*.

When texts feel hospitable, response and recognition come easily. Readers feel invited to participate in vicarious social worlds. Readers feel drawn to images in some texts and respond with a sense of openness and inquiry to this addressivity, a sense of wanting to be there and an anticipation of belonging as a participant in the meanings being offered. Other times, readers might feel that the characters and places are not inviting and the relational invitations are less known or even unknown. In this case, readers may listen with more caution, taking in a little at a time, titrating what is new and different, or staying "outside" of the storied world altogether. Teachers can support children's relational comprehending by finding hospitable texts for their young readers, and by accompanying them into those texts that might feel less welcoming through side-by-side reading and interactive read-alouds.

Response

In the simplest sense, response is what happens when readers first encounter the representations of texts. Response is an opening move toward the storied world that occurs when readers perceive and apprehend symbolic representations. Something of the reader responds—and proceeds toward— the addressivity of the text. Responses are not random (Bakhtin, 1981), but rather are communicative actions specific to someone about something (Linell, 2009). In this case, response is the communication between the subjectivities of the reader and those represented in the text. As we saw in Chapter 3, young children's initial responses to wordless books are often significantly embodied. They use gaze and gesture to respond to the presence of text and locate themselves in relation to it. They begin their relationship with the storied world. Children also use their bodies and words to express their stance toward the text, their willingness to read, and their feelings about the anticipated encounter.

Recognition

Recognition often follows immediately on the heels of response. Readers notice something about the text that reminds them of themselves, their experiences, and their world. When readers identify similarities between themselves and the text world, this recognition serves as an entryway into the storied world. Recognition begins the reader–text transaction, a critical part of comprehending.

Recognition is a comprehending activity that involves the reader's awareness of complex experiences as represented and lived in the reader's consciousness. James Gee (2001) refers to the resources that readers can become aware of and later use (via *recontextualization*) in their encounters with text as "situatedness." Gee describes the makeup of situatedness as follows: "These experiences, perceptions, feelings, actions, interactions are stored in the mind or brain . . . something like dynamic images tied to perception of the world and our own bodies, internal states and feelings" (p. 715). This situatedness is what readers become aware of, perceive, feel, and move forward as they begin their encounter with text. When readers recognize themselves in the text, they not only think and reason about knowledge by asking, "What do I already know that will connect me to the text?" they also perceive, feel, and intuit similarities between their own languaged experiences and what they apprehend in the text, all of which moves them forward in their sense-making. Recognition, then, is reflective activity which requires a look at oneself. In order to see something that is like oneself in a text, readers first glance at themselves and their understanding of themselves. The text acts as a kind of mirror. As readers encounter it, they become aware of themselves in its light.

Recognition, like response, occurs quickly and is largely intuitive. Readers are often unaware of this part of their sense-making. Recognition may happen quickly, but it does not happen automatically. Both readers and texts influence when and how it occurs. Because recognition initially involves an awareness of something about oneself, it is dependent upon and afforded by an openness to vulnerability. This awareness brings to light memories, thoughts, emotions, and embodiments of experiences, which may not always be comfortable. But as we noted earlier, texts also matter. Readers may experience the set of meanings offered by texts as unfamiliar, something outside of their range of experiences. Sometimes this can be experienced by readers as difficult and forced, as if the text were pressing in from the outside, asking them to be something they are not. Of course, this can thwart sense-making. While the need for recognition as part of comprehension is important, pairing texts with readers on this basis is not as simple as lining up experiences or backgrounds. Though these elements should be considered, individual readers do things with texts and imagine connections that teachers and others on the "outside" can't always see. Observing children as they read wordless books and making note of recognition activity as we do in this chapter can be helpful in this regard.

Recontextualization

Recontextualization moves what is recognized into the narrative world. Readers, having made an initial response and recognized something in the text, can now situate that part of themselves (i.e., their experiences, emotions, and language) in the text world. Recontextualization requires imagination and emotion even more so than recognition. When readers recontextualize experience, they don't simply use their background knowledge to objectively connect fact A of themselves to fact B in a text. They instead form connections—relationships—between their experiences and the perceived experiences represented in the text. This merger requires imagining those relationships into being, bringing into one time and space the readers' sense of their own lives and being with what they encounter in the text. Zittoun (2016) puts it this way when referring to the connections people make during sense-making with each other in actual worlds: "Sense is thus emotional and demands the creation of 'connections' between a given object and one's overall present and past experience" (p. 3).

These imagined relationships between readers and texts create something new, what Rosenblatt (1978) calls the "poem." The imaginative activity that creates these relationships with text is central to children's comprehending. In the case of wordless book reading, this new text is voiced during reading and provides a window into this aspect of comprehending. Dyson (1999) describes recontextualization in children's writing: "We learn our words from particular people in particular places and then we recontextualize them, and given the strength of our own intentions we revoice them" (p. 369). During reading, children use the strength of their intentions to recontextualize and revoice experiences in dialogue with narrative worlds—thereby creating a new text. Recontextualization and its voicing demonstrate the coauthoring of comprehending text.

Response, recognition, and recontextualization are comprehending activities during which children's subjectivities emerge and are imaginatively enacted in their encounters with peopled narrative worlds. Each contributes to children's movement into those worlds and their relational participation within them. These activities function as living artifacts of comprehending as well as the enacted, story-situated personhood of readers.

AMBER AND CAMELLA

Amber and Camella differ greatly in how they use response, recognition, and recontextualization during comprehending as represented by these readings. It is important to remember that these comprehending activities will not look precisely the same when these same readers encounter different texts at different times, and so these readings offer but one example of how these comprehending activities unfold for Amber and Camella. As we will see in Chapter 7, multiple readings across texts can be useful in garnering a fuller picture of children's developing comprehension. Still, like every meaning-making moment we are privileged to know, children's readings can be instructive and shape our ability to nurture that meaning-making through teaching.

Amber is White and was nearly 5½ at the time she read *I Had Measles* to me in a small room adjacent to her classroom, during the fall of her kindergarten year at one of the Early Learning Centers. She appeared somewhat shy and initially needed prompting as she held the book open for me to see. With each page turn, she showed me the pictures and looked at me, as if seeking affirmation.

Camella is Black and was 5½ in the spring of her pre-K year when she read *I Had Measles* in a quiet classroom of the Head Start preschool. Camella was talkative and eager to read. She exuded a sense of confidence and opened the book with anticipation, independence, and energy, all of which she maintained throughout the reading. She sustained a storyteller's approach to the reading, with a few side comments about the book and her experiences.

Both Amber and Camella read *I Had Measles*, a story about a family where one of the children is sick, described more fully in Chapter 1. As with all transcripts, you can find Amber and Camella's transcripts in the online resources for this chapter (see online Appendix 4.A at www.tcpress.com).

Response, Recognition, and Recontextualization in Amber's Reading

Amber had a hesitant response to this wordless book reading. She was very quiet, seemed unsure about what was happening, and at the same time wanted to please. Having not had the chance to observe Amber in the classroom, I wondered if her hesitance was characteristic of her approach to reading. While a hesitant stance can come from a range of sources, my experience with children in schools made me think about the possibility that Amber was worried about doing this reading "right" and might constrain her engagement in sense-making. As Cambourne (1995) described in his conditions for language learning, children's sense of being able to succeed in a language event can be crucial to the achievement of that success.

Once Amber settled into the idea that she could participate in this reading, her response took on more of a sense of inquiry—the text was something to figure out. She would silently take in the images, apprehending them as if they were material to work with. Her narration did not come quickly or spontaneously. After studying and narrating a page, she would show that page to me as a teacher would do in a read-aloud. Then she would look up at me with a smile.

She begins on page 2, which shows the sick child in bed rubbing her eyes, and a younger child and a lively puppy seem to be waking her up. Amber reads, "I Had Measles," repeating the title as I had just stated it for her, as if choosing a beginning that she knew couldn't be wrong. Despite the presence of three characters and something happening between them, she repeats the title. Turning the page, Amber scans and studies the images. On the left-hand side, a woman, meant to be the mother, has her hand on the sick child's spotted belly. The right-hand side depicts a new narrative event: the woman and younger child appear to be leaving the room where the sick child is now sound asleep. Amber reads, "He got bumps." Again, despite the presence of multiple characters and two sets of actions, Amber limits her reading to a descriptive statement about one character. Her reading continues: "He's taking his temperature. He's drinking juice. He's laying down. He's looking outside. He is coloring."

For Amber, recognition is related to "school reading." Participating in a school-related reading genre and "figuring out" the text seemed to constrain her emotional connection and her ability to be present to the text. Her hesitant response to my expectation that she would read *I Had Measles* independently seemed to lead to her recontextualization of a school reading experience and the anticipation of relational support. Throughout the reading, her interest remained on sharing the book with me and seeking support, rather than dialogically engaging the text herself as a primary way of participating. She would smile frequently, expressing a sense of comfort with this school-related participation genre.

Recontextualization of school reading genres is also evident in the reading itself. If we examine her narrative, Amber also seems to recontexualize her experience with the controlled texts commonly used for guided reading in her kindergarten classroom. Though she studies the illustrations carefully and does not rush her reading, she narrates in short sentences that are grammatically similar. Every utterance in her reading has a subject–verb construction beginning with "He's." Interestingly, once she read the first two pages, her narrating quickened. Recontextualizing the comfortable familiarity of repetitive text gave her the support she needed (see Table 4.1).

Entering the narrative social world seems difficult, or at best uninteresting, for Amber. Amber does not allow her own subjectivity into the text. For example, Amber does not name characters. Giving characters identities necessarily means recognizing similarities between oneself and the storied world and then recontextualizing relevant personal experiences in that world—even if it is simply naming characters with familial identities. This makes naming characters an important indicator of relational involvement in story, and something to notice in terms of comprehending. Instead, Amber sticks with the pronoun "he" throughout the reading, even using it to refer to the different male and female characters. It isn't clear why Amber does this, though it could be said it is a "safe" strategy for dealing with the ambiguity of this text and staying "outside" the story by not responding to multiple different genders. Keeping the gender male might also feel safe since it makes identification with the character less likely.

The characters Amber constructs are involved in action only, and those actions are closely linked to the images in the text. She stays in this landscape of action, leaving aside the landscape of consciousness (Bruner, 1986); characters' thoughts, feelings, and engagement with each other are all invisible. Action may be easier to perceive, respond to, and recontextualize. Indeed, the actions she uses in her narration are common to childhood. The fact that we don't know much about the characters or the world of *I Had Measles* from Amber's narrative suggests that she is not recontextualizing these details of her human experience to enact characters or settings, or that she doesn't think voicing her own experience is part of reading. This approach confines her meaning-making.

Table 4.1. Recognition and Recontextualization in Amber's Reading of *I Had Measles*

School reading genres	Shares the book with me like a read-aloud
Book genre	Repetitive sentence structure overrides sense-making

Amber's comprehending activities seem constrained by her response and recontextualization of a school-related reading genre that guides her expectations of what reading is and how she should do it. Rather than situating herself within the story world through recontextualization, she situates the participation genres of read-aloud and guided reading, resulting in a relationally sparse, linguistically simple reading. Amber may not believe or have had the experience that reading involves her. Instead, she regards it as something to be figured out and "done," like "doing school." On the other hand, Amber may not experience this text as hospitable, or feel addressed by the images, which would also limit her response and recognition.

Responding to Amber

Observing Amber and analyzing her wordless book reading offers a starting point for response. First, Amber's initial response—her posture and frequent eye contact—indicate that her view of reading is social. Because Amber appears hesitant, a caring relational stance in which a teacher or other adult carefully engages with her meaning-making will likely help her be more present to the texts she reads and use her imagination to recognize and recontextualize her comprehending. Though beginning a reading conversation with appreciation and affirmation is always recommended, in Amber's case it seems critical.

> Thank you for reading *I Had Measles* to me, Amber. You noticed so many things that were happening in this story and I could tell you really wanted to share them with me. Is there a place in the book you'd like to show me or talk about?

After appreciating and authentically affirming some aspect of her reading and inviting her to lead by showing me a place in the book of her choice, I might move to talking with her about how she seems to spend time studying the details of pictures, but then narrates quite simply. A possible response could sound like this:

> Amber, you are really studying the pictures in this book. I bet you noticed a lot of different things in those pictures. Are there some things that you

noticed but didn't say out loud when you read the story? Can you show
me where that might have happened?

This kind of conversation could provide a social space outside of the
reading in which Amber could voice some of the connections she may have
been making silently. Drawing out responses through conversation may
help Amber recognize and recontextualize herself and her experiences with
and within the text. Encouraging Amber to reread *I Had Measles* using
more of what she may have voiced in conversation gives Amber permission
to take charge of the reading and use her own response to make meaning.
Of course, as always, drawing Amber out in conversation and asking her to
revisit parts of the story she may have left out has to be done in a way that
doesn't feel like correction. Rather, I would want to respond to Amber's
view of reading as social by inviting a back-and-forth conversation in which
she talks about other things she may have noticed and I respond like a col-
laborator in meaning-making.

As mentioned earlier, Amber may experience this particular text as in-
hospitable to invitations for a relationship. Trying other wordless texts with
Amber would tell us more about her comprehending activities and the kinds
of texts that prompt her recognition and recontextualization of a broader
range of experiences, as well as her imagination. A conversation with Amber about the text could provide helpful information.

You know, Amber, I wonder how you felt about this book. Do you think it
was a bit hard to read? Would you like to try a different wordless book?

In addition, a verbal observation of the short sentences she used, which
sounded like the guided reading books in her classroom, could release her
from this genre inhibition:

Amber, your story sounded so much like a little book I know, where there
is one sentence on every page and the sentences kind of sound the same.
Did you think about that kind of book when you were reading?

Amber may be unaware that she is recontextualizing a reading genre.
She certainly may be unaware that it is constraining her sense-making and
making it difficult for her to accept the invitations of this storied world.
Talking with her about different kinds of stories and purposes for reading
may give her permission to use her imagination to recognize and recontextualize her own experiences. For example, a conversation in which a
leveled book is studied alongside a wordless book or picture book could
help Amber see that she can make sense of texts differently because of what
they offer her.

Let's look at this little book together. When we read this book, there are
just a few things happening on each page. But, wow, look at this one.
There are lots of things happening here, and several different characters. I
wonder who they are. I wonder if they know each other or are in the same
family, and why they are doing the things we see in the pictures. Isn't it
interesting and kind of fun to notice how different books make us think
differently?

Overall, a relational response, rather than a purposefully instructional
one, seems best for Amber. A caring teacher can assure Amber that she
is a person meant for reading and that forming relationships with texts is
what readers do. Such assurance may help her be present to texts, form
relationships within storied words, and voice her sense-making with more
confidence. This may be particularly important for Amber since, as noted
earlier, the vulnerability of reading requires a certain risk, particularly when
learning to read and trying to do things "right."

Finally, I would want to provide Amber with independent experiences
of a range of different texts to enhance the probability that she will experience herself as an empowered, imaginative, emotional, and dialogically
engaged reader. If, in fact, it becomes clear that she has typical guided reading texts in mind, this would lead me to some decisions about her reading
experiences. First, I would want Amber (like all children) to have a broad
range of books available to her in order to experience rich, complex stories.
Second, I would want her to have more experiences with wordless books.
Reading more wordless texts with Amber could help her gain confidence in
her abilities to engage in meaning-making with texts. Once she lets go of her
commitment to what sounds "right" in terms of narration, the absence of
print and opportunities for choosing from and enacting multiple meanings
from images could help her gain confidence as a reader.

Response, Recognition, and Recontextualization in Camella's Reading

Camella's reading of *I Had Measles* offers another unique example of a
child's use of response, recognition, and recontextualization in comprehending. Unlike Amber, Camella displayed an eagerness in her reading of *I Had
Measles*. She was physically active most of the time. She moved her hands
and feet, pushed back her hair, and gestured regularly. She was a young
reader decidedly full of energy. Camella approached the reading openly and
seemed to regard the text as a place to explore and be herself.

Camella blends response, recognition, and recontextualization throughout her reading of *I Had Measles* (see Table 4.2). At the very start, when
looking at the title page, Camella says, "Look at the little puppy. I got that
little puppy." Camella recognizes the puppy as something she has—a fairly

straightforward personal response. Camella doesn't say that she has a puppy *like* that one, but that she has *that* puppy. She has literally put some aspect of her life into the storied world. On the first page, after a brief continuation of this association with her own dog, she returns to the text: "The, the girl and, and the boy and the dog was sleepin'. And she was sick. And she had to stay home, just like me, like, like Spring Break and, and um . . . " In this utterance, Camella reads the illustration and names the characters, calling them simply the girl, the boy, and the dog. She goes on to recognize this as something that happened to her and to recontextualize her own experience, "she had to stay home, just like me." Given that this is a wordless book, there is no narration telling the reader that the child has to stay home. Though this may seem obvious, not all young readers make "staying home" part of their sense-making of *I Had Measles*.

Camella continues her use of recontextualization later in the story. Page 4 depicts a woman leaning over the sick child, who is in bed and has a thermometer in her mouth. On page 5 there is a male character holding stuffed animals, a doll, and what looks like a glass of juice. Camella reads: "And the dad, and the dad had got the toys, but she had a really bad sickness. I got better when I had a really bad sickness. And they was, and they, and she had to stay forever and ever, until she feel better."

Camella had, in fact, been very ill. She recognizes and recontextualizes that experience as part of the story. She even adds, "I got better when I had a really bad sickness," which moves her briefly outside of the story. In her next utterance, "And they was, and they, and she had to stay forever and ever, until she feel better," she recontextualizes her own experience of having to stay in bed for a long time until she recovered from her illness. Her imaginative recontextualization allows her to author details of what is happening in *I Had Measles*: "she had to stay forever [. . .] until she feel better."

Later in the story, Camella continues to recontextualize her own experience. On page 5 the sick child is sleeping in bed in the background. In the foreground, the younger sibling is crouched just outside the door with his arms around the puppy. Camella reads:

> The brother said, "She gotta stay at home for ALL day, until she be better for school." So the brother got ready for school and her dog, like when I come to school, I'll hug my dog. I got that dog. And he's, and um, yeah. And he always, and he always runs to me.

Camella uses her experiences to imagine that the younger sibling is a brother and that he has gotten ready for school while the sick child sleeps. She then returns to her own experience and likens hugging her dog to what the character appears to be doing in the illustration. She adds, "And he always, and he always runs to me."

Still later in the story, the sick child appears to be trying to get out of bed. The mother has entered the room and is walking toward the child, one hand outstretched and the other held up with her right hand facing the closed curtain (earlier in the story the mother had closed the curtain). Camella reads:

> And the mother had said, she had closed the curtain, so, so no light won't get in her way 'cause when, when the light get in my way I been closing it. Like with, my curtains always fall, my granny always fix it back. When [Camella] do something, when she get bad, then she do this, cover her face up. And um. So she said, "I'll close the curtains." And, and she had jumped out of bed but her mom said, "Stay in bed."

Again, Camella blends response, recognition, and recontextualization in her comprehending of this text. First, she returns to the earlier event of the book when the mother closed the curtain and explains why this happened: "so, so no light won't get in her way." She then responds to this event, which she has already recontextualized, adding, "When the light get in my way I been closing it. Like with, my curtains always fall, my granny always fix it back."

Camella then extends this response by turning it into its own narrative in an oral storytelling style: "When [Camella] do something, when she get bad, then she do this, cover her face up." Then, with only an "um" to resituate herself within the story, she continues reading, "So she said, 'I'll close the curtains.' And, and she had jumped out of bed but her mom said, 'Stay in bed.'"

Camella has returned fully to being in the story and imagining what the mother would say as the sick girl tries to get out of bed, perhaps using her own experience again to make sense of the illustration.

Camella's unique merger of response, recognition, and recontextualization yields a lively, intricate, and coauthored text of personal meaning, emotion, and imagination. Rather than recontextualizing a school-situated reading experience using repetition as Amber did, Camella recontextualizes the participation genre of oral storytelling that is infused with personal comments and anecdotes. Recontextualizing an oral storytelling genre gives Camella a way to participate in the book reading genre of *I Had Measles*, and supports the active use of personal response and recontextualization of her own experiences. The insertion of personal anecdotes and imaginative connections that Camella creates between the world of *I Had Measles* and her own experiences might be seen as distracting from the story's intended meaning, resulting in a less focused rendering. Indeed, Camella's reading has qualities of African American vernacular which have been historically stigmatized and undervalued. For example, Applebee (1985) referred to this

Table 4.2. Examples of Response and Recontextualization in Camella's Reading of *I Had Measles*

Recognition	Recognizes story as something she knows and knows how to tell
	Recognizes the puppy as her dog
	Recognizes illness as something she has experienced
Recontextualization	Recontextualizes her experience of being sick
	Recontextualizes family experiences
	Recontextualizes experiences of having a dog
	Recontextualizes storytelling style
Merger of response, recognition, recontextualization	And she had to stay home, just like me, like, like Spring Break and, and um . . .
	And that dog always jump on me, but he didn't even make me fall.

kind of narration as an "unfocused chain." Yet it is precisely Camella's ability to recontextualize personal experience within *I Had Measles* that allows her to joyfully and energetically make sense of this storied world. Wordless book reading provides a hospitable space for personal sense-making in which her storying style is decidedly a strength.

To sum up, Camella responds to *I Had Measles* as a place for her to tell a story. She believes that reading this book has something to do with *her*. Camella recognizes and immediately voices her recognition of the puppy. This gives her immediate entrance to the storied world, which she finds hospitable. She is an active agent who brings her subjectivities to the act of comprehending and engages dialogically with and within the story world. Camella recontextualizes her own experiences and uses them to invent narrative elements; she has become a coauthor. Her imaginative engagement within the storied world results in a lively narrative filled with characters, situations, and experiences.

Responding to Camella

Camella's emotional and imaginative involvement in comprehending *I Had Measles* is what is most striking (and enjoyable!) about her reading. She is engaged dialogically and emotionally from the outset with her recognition of the puppy on the title page. This engagement fuels her meaning-making. Her comprehending is also very imaginative, in terms of her recontextualization of personal experience and the oral storytelling genre to elaborate her reading. Her emotional connection and imaginative approach are central to the ways in which she uses response, recognition, and recontextualization in her meaning-making. These strengths make good talking points for a reading conversation. After an appreciative comment and invitation as in other reading conversations, I might continue by saying something like this:

> Camella, you seemed to really connect to this book from the very beginning when you recognized the puppy. That recognition of the puppy really seemed to help you get moving into your reading. Grown-up readers do the same kind of thing. They recognize parts of their lives, even who they are, in the books they read and it helps them understand the books as they read. So what you did here in this story is pretty important.
>
> Another thing I noticed about your reading is how you used your own experiences to understand this book. For example, you mentioned that you had a really bad sickness in your reading. On this page you read, "And the dad, and the dad had got the toys, but she had a really bad sickness. I got better when I had a really bad sickness. And they was, and they, and she had to stay forever and ever, until she feel better." Can you tell me more about what you were thinking here, when you were reading this page? What were you remembering that helped you know how to read this page?

There are many other places where Camella recontextualizes her experiences, but at this point I would move to talking with her about her storytelling style.

> Camella, one thing I really enjoyed and found myself thinking about when you were reading are the little stories you put into the bigger story of *I Had Measles*. Let me show you. On this page, you read, "Like with, my curtains always fall, my granny always fix it back. When Camella do something, when she get bad, then she do this, cover her face up." It almost seemed like you were about to tell a new story! Do you like to tell stories? Can you tell me how the stories you hear help you with the stories you read?

As always, it is important that these small reading conversations with young children about what they do as meaning-makers when reading wordless books do not become too long or academic. Rather, to notice lovingly what they are doing in terms of the comprehending activities of response, recognition, and recontextualization, shows children that you are aware of how they *are* with books—how their comprehending is personal, emotional, and imaginative.

Table 4.3. Amber and Camella's Responses to *I Had Measles*

Amber	Quiet, shy, unsure	Storied text as space to figure out and get right
Camella	Cheerful, active, eager, confident	Storied text as a space to "be in," a social space where I can be me
		Story as a place to perform, invent, and have fun

WHAT RESPONSE, RECOGNITION, AND RECONTEXTUALIZATION CONTRIBUTE TO COMPREHENDING

Amber and Camella demonstrate the potential potency of response in comprehending (see Table 4.3). Response is the necessary moment of emerging subjectivity in face of the text, the "here I am!" that can happen as readers are addressed by texts and respond with their presence. For Amber, being present to the text is constrained by what she thinks reading should be and her recontextualization of a controlled text genre limits the potential recognition and response on her part. Amber doesn't seem to draw on her imagination and remains outside of the storied world. Sensitive, nonjudging response can support Amber in being more comfortable making her own meanings as she reads, and exposure to a wide range of different kinds of texts can enhance her sense of what stories are. As noted earlier, collaborative meaning-making, either in individual side-by-side reading or in group interactive read-alouds, in which Amber is encouraged and supported in being a contributor, could also support Amber's reading development.

However, as we see in Camella's reading, a fuller, emotionally driven response facilitates recognition and recontextualization, which moves her further into the storied world to form relationships and enact meanings. Wordless book reading, as an open image-based meaning-making event, provides a culturally responsive practice for personal sense-making in which Camella's storying style contributes substantially to comprehending. An extended response to Camella's wordless book readings, which I return to in Chapter 8, would be to audiorecord and write out her stories, so that her storytelling can be more widely appreciated within her classroom community.

When readers recontextualize languaged experiences into text worlds, they begin to make sense of those worlds. With the illustrator, they coauthor as they relate the personal and text worlds in meaningful ways. Recontextualization is the means by which meaning happens neither in the reader nor text alone, but in the transaction (Rosenblatt, 2004). Not only are readers constructing and creating a new text world, they are simultaneously

reconstructing and recreating who they are as text-related, text-situated beings every time they read. In this way, though not always immediately apparent, comprehending is a selfing process (Bruder, 1998) that contributes
to the development of the person reading (Ivey & Johnston, 2016; Lysaker,
2002).

Recognition and recontextualization are imaginative comprehending
activities that involve movement from the "here and now" into and around
the "there and then" of text worlds and can contribute to the beautiful
experience of being in storied worlds that motivates and inspires lifelong
reading. Paying attention to young children's response, recognition, and recontextualization as they make sense of wordless books allows us to see,
value, and respond to these critical relational aspects of comprehending that
go unnoticed in prompted assessments of emergent reading comprehension,
which might ask children to simply name characters or identify the setting.
Instead, in wordless books reading, we can notice and value the activities of
response, recognition, and recontextualization during which children make
the meaning of characters their own—a central quality of mature and satis-
fying reading. As we will see in the next chapter, recognition and recontextualization are the beginning of a set of imaginative activities that contribute
to and deepen children's comprehending.

CHAPTER 5

Comprehending as Relationship with Text
Social Imagination, Narrative Imagination, and Intersubjectivity

In this chapter we will continue to notice and respond to relational aspects of children's comprehending, remembering that, as relational activities, these too are grounded in emotion, fueled by imagination, and influenced by the texts themselves. In this chapter we meet Lenya and James, about a year apart in age, both eager and lively readers of wordless texts.

SOCIAL IMAGINATION, NARRATIVE IMAGINATION, AND INTERSUBJECTIVE ENACTMENT

We might say that response, recognition, and recontextualization—through imaginative moves into storied worlds—are somewhat reader centered. It is the reader's response, the recognition of something like the reader in the text, and the recontextualization of the reader's experience that constitute these initial relational moves. This initial relational activity effectively lands children within the storied world where the dialogic transaction that is critical to comprehending begins. Social and narrative imagination, on the other hand, while enacted by readers and involving sense-making processes, have more to do with the storied world itself and its landscapes of consciousness and action.

Once children have recontextualized their experiences as they encounter text, they become part of the peopled narrative world and begin to move around in and make sense of it. Part of that sense-making has to do with characters' thoughts, feelings, intentions, and beliefs—their inner worlds. As noted earlier, Jerome Bruner (1986) refers to this as the "landscape of consciousness." Social imagination is when children imagine what characters are thinking, feeling, believing, or intending (Ivey & Johnston, 2013; Johnston, 1993; Lysaker, 2012, 2014; Lysaker et al., 2011). Another part of comprehending storied worlds, and closely related to social imagination, is making sense of more concrete aspects of story, like action and setting, which, as we know, Bruner refers to as the "landscape of action." Narrative imagination is when children invent aspects of narrative within this landscape of action in order to make sense of the story (Lysaker & Hopper, 2015). Narrative imagination differs from the more traditional inference in that it involves leaving text-implied meanings behind or even refuting them in support of one's own sense-making. Children's use of social and narrative imagination during reading engages them in deep dialogicality within the text world. Rosenblatt (1978) would say their sense-making of text is now "lived experience." Imagining the inner worlds and realities of characters can lead readers to fully experience the storied world as they connect with the people and events of that world. To do this is to achieve a sense of sharedness or cobeing with the people and places of the vicarious social world of the text (Lysaker & Wessel-Powell, in press), what I refer to as *enacted intersubjectivity*.

LENYA AND JAMES

In this chapter we meet Lenya and James. Lenya is Black, was just short of 5½ years old, and was attending the Head Start Preschool when we read *When Jack Goes Out* together. James, a White boy, was nearly 6½.
and at the end of his kindergarten year in one of the Early Learning Centers when he read *I Had Measles* with me. James was just beginning to decode simple printed texts. Full transcripts of their readings can be found in the online resources for this chapter (see online Appendixes 5.A and 5.B at www.tcpress.com).

Social Imagination, Narrative Imagination, and Intersubjective Enactment in Lenya's Reading

Lenya and I met at the Reading Table in a small room adjacent to the Head Start Preschool classrooms. She spent a minute looking through the books, picking up, and putting down several before saying, "Ooh, I would read this one!" She held up *When Jack Goes Out* for me to see. She seemed enthusiastic and emotionally connected to this choice, as if she recognized something or remembered something of interest or delight from a prior encounter. As it turned out, she had not read it before and told me that she didn't even have it in her classroom. Knowing Lenya, the chance to read something brand new may have triggered her excitement.

   Lenya begins narrating upon opening the book by using the endpapers. She starts like a good storyteller: "Once upon a time, Jack went out to play." A simple start with multiple possibilities for what might happen next. Then Lenya reads, "Jack had to go to his house, his playhouse, to go to sleep." Using "had to" rather than simply "went" adds intentionality. There is now purpose to the underlying action. Jack *had to go*—for some reason. Lenya does this again on the next page, the title page, by reading, "At night the little girl *had to go* to sleep in the real house and the Jack went out."

While the difference between action with and without intention may seem a small and perhaps unimportant point in terms of Lenya's comprehending, imagine the opening of her story without it: "Jack went out to play. Jack went to his house, his playhouse to go to sleep. At night the little girl went to sleep in the real house." By using "had to" Lenya has opened up the landscape of consciousness, in which there are *reasons* behind actions—thoughts and feelings that make those actions happen—and not actions alone, though Lenya does not articulate these reasons. This part of Lenya's comprehending seems linked to her recontextualization of familial experiences, in which children often "have to" go to sleep. She has made assumptions about this storied world, having recontextualized purposeful human experiences, imagined the intentionality of characters' actions (an example of social imagination), and created a delicate, nearly imperceptible, intersubjective tone (Garte, 2016) as part of the activity of comprehending. In terms of her comprehending, these assumptions and her use of social imagination make her an active part of the storied world.

Lenya continues to enact social imagination by giving thoughts to characters. The title page shows a young child in pajamas walking toward a house at night and Jack the dog is tied up to his chain at the doghouse. On the first full-page spread, the image shows Jack with his head down, eyes lowered, and walking around his doghouse. Responding to this image, and the prior one, Lenya gives the identity of "sister" to the young child who has gone into the house, and imagines that the dog is thinking about her. She reads, "And Jack was thinking about his sister." This is an unusual enactment of meaning since humans don't have dogs as siblings. In fact, Lenya hesitates and for a moment looks uncharacteristically doubtful as she sits with the idea that she has created a sibling relationship between Jack (the dog) and the girl going in the house. Lenya sticks with her sense-making as if the notion that there is a relationship here is what is most important. At this point in the story, Jack is at his doghouse for the night and the little girl is going in to her house for the night as well. In this reading, it seems that what focuses and leads Lenya's sense-making is their relationship, even to the point of rejecting and replacing conventional thinking about sibling relationships. Her enactment of social imagination revolving around characters and their relationships leads her to create a sibling relationship between the dog and the child, inventing a new element—an act of narrative imagination. Like Camella in Chapter 4, her comprehending is a creative event of coauthoring.

The story moves forward and the space monsters arrive. Lenya reads, "Jack saw the space monsters. Jack was scared." This is a clear example of Lenya's imagining the feelings of a character and enacting them in her comprehending. She continues, "The monsters was coming to eat him and he should go in the house and be safe." Lenya again imagines a narrative element not present in the text: the monsters want to eat him (there is no such indication in the images). Her imagining that the monsters want to eat Jack may certainly involve her recontextualization of experiences from other stories, TV, or movies. However, this moment of narrative imagining is tied closely to her construction of Jack as "scared," as is her next utterance of "and he should go in the house and be safe." Her work within the intersubjective landscape of consciousness leads her to create a reason for Jack's fear: The monsters want to eat him. Imagining characters' inner worlds inspires Lenya to create actions connected to those inner worlds or narrative imagination.

Lenya's story is also full of emotion, which is linked to her involvement in the intersubjective world of the characters where she enacts thoughts, feelings, and intentions. The intonation of her voice reveals the state of emotional investment that imbues her comprehending activity. On one page Jack is shown in a pond with the space monsters after being unhooked from the doghouse. Lenya reads, "Then Jack came to a horrible river!" as if Jack were experiencing a real calamity. In the image Jack's head is barely above water and he looks a little surprised by his circumstance. Lenya interprets that this is a "horrible river" and not a calm pond with children's toys floating in it as depicted (i.e., another instance of narrative imagination). While there is water in the image on this page, her enactment of emotion through inflection comes from her imaginative sense of the danger Jack is experiencing, leading Lenya to create this "horrible river."

Later in the story, when the monsters hook Jack back up to the doghouse, the image depicts him as a little sad. Lenya reads, "He is worried about his sister. It was time for him to go." Her voice is soft and drops at the end of the utterance, as if she is experiencing the character's feelings. Lenya remains true to the relationship she has invented between Jack and the sister, imagining the worry and sadness of their separation (i.e., the sister is still in the house while Jack is outside). While it might make more sense to an adult mind to imagine the sister worrying about Jack, Lenya gives Jack—the central character—greater agency. In addition, it seems that it is the ongoing relationships of characters as well as their feelings that engage Lenya during her comprehending activity.

Toward the end of the story, the little girl (sister) comes outside. Though Jack is in plain sight in the illustration, Lenya reads with intensity, "Where's Jack? Where's Jack? It's probably the monsters took him." Lenya is once again enacting, and this time voicing, the thoughts of the little girl: "Where's Jack?" Lenya is also creating a narrative element—that Jack is missing. It is as if Lenya, being emotionally involved in the story, has imagined that the space monsters *did* take Jack, despite evidence to the contrary in the images. Lenya creates a narrative element to satisfy her own lived experience of the story.

There are two final places where Lenya's comprehending involves social imagination. Both times she voices the thoughts of the little girl by saying, "And where's his collar? Where's his leash? He forgot to keep his leash." These expressions of surprise and confusion on the part of the character show that Lenya is imagining the characters' thoughts. This intersubjective involvement adds depth to the character. Lenya has consistently created an emotionally imbued, intersubjective landscape of consciousness through social imagination.

Overall, Lenya's reading of *When Jack Goes Out* is highly imaginative. Her recontextualization of familial relationships and emotions lead her to make certain assumptions about the storied world, an important part of her comprehending. These assumptions guide her enactment of intersubjectivity. For Lenya, this assumption that meanings can be shared between her personal world and the world of story happens quickly and easily as part of her sense-making of this text and seems an automatic part of her comprehending. One result of Lenya's assumption of shared meanings is an intersubjective narrative climate with emotionally imbued relationships. She further develops this relational dialogicality between herself and the storied world, as well as between characters within it, as she enacts relationships through social imagination. She also creates new narrative elements through narrative imagination to accommodate her relational constructions.

From this reading and careful thinking about Lenya's comprehending work, we can see that her use of social and narrative imagination contribute to her comprehending in important ways (see Table 5.1). They allow Lenya to: (1) situate herself in the vicarious social world of story as coauthor; (2) enact relationships between characters and voice their thoughts and feelings; (3) invent new narrative elements that make sense with her enactment of characters and their relationships; (4) create an emotion-filled landscape of consciousness; and (5) enact intersubjectivity between her understandings and the storied world.

Responding to Lenya. Observing Lenya's uses of social and narrative imagination as well as intersubjective enactment give us several talking points for a reading conversation about her comprehending. As always, I would begin with an authentic appreciation. In this instance, I would want to respond to her emotionally voiced, imaginative story by saying something like:

> Lenya, the way you read the story of *When Jack Goes Out* really had me captivated. I really enjoyed it.

I might then take this further by exploring some of her imaginative world:

> You know, one thing I noticed is that you started the story right away by creating a relationship between Jack and the little girl. You said she was

Table 5.1. Examples of Social Imagination, Narrative Imagination, and Intersubjective Enactment in Lenya's Reading of *When Jack Goes Out*

Social imagination and intersubjective enactment	Imagining thoughts, intentions, feelings, and relationships	He was thinking about his sister.
		Jack was worried about his sister.
		Jack was scared.
		He had to go to sleep in his playhouse.
		She had to go to sleep in her real house.
Narrative imagination	Creating new narrative elements	The sibling relationships between Jack and "his sister."
		Then Jack came in a horrible river.
		It was so deep deep down.
		And then the girl went outside and where's Jack? Where's Jack? It's probably the monsters took him.

his sister. Can you tell me a little about that? Was there something you were remembering or something in the pictures that made you think about the story this way?

This would lead to a conversation about this aspect of her comprehending, which stands out as imaginative. In this line of exploration, I would also explore Lenya's use of intentionality. Of course, this is an abstract concept that can be discussed with young children in terms of actual experiences. For example, it might be useful to say:

Lenya, in your reading you said that Jack *had to* go to his house to sleep and that the girl *had to* go to her real house to sleep. That seemed important to your story. I was wondering why they had to. Can you talk to me about that?

This might elicit stories of experience of having to go to bed in her own life, or the importance of a being in a safe place at night when you sleep. I would affirm for Lenya that when adult readers make sense of stories, they often use their own experiences of the world to help them understand. It is important to reiterate that this is not the application of specific background experience, but rather recontextualizing previous participation in the world *as experienced* into the storied world. It is embodied and emotionally charged. I would continue by exploring her use of social imagination and asking her about the two parts where Jack was "thinking about" and "worried about" his sister:

> Lenya, Jack was doing some thinking and having lots of feelings in your reading. On this page, where Jack is walking around looking at the ground, you read, "Jack was thinking about his sister." Can you tell me more about your thinking here?

As a teacher or researcher interested in her comprehending, I would also want to talk with Lenya about her narrative inventions, particularly at times when she displays heightened investment. Her narration about the river and Jack losing his collar and leash are full of intense emotional intonations and examples of this investment. I would respond as follows:

> You know, Lenya, I really noticed two parts of your story where you seemed to be very involved. Your voice went up, your eyes got wide. Do you know where I mean? (This opens up the possibility for Lenya to share her own thoughts about her reading.) I was thinking of two places. First, when Jack was swimming and you said there was a "horrible river" that was "so deep deep." Can you talk about that part? Let's go to that page.

The purpose of looking at the image again is not to have Lenya revise her meaning to match the text. Rather, I would use the images to provide memory support, so that I could hear more of her sense-making about this part of the story. In a similar way, I would explore with Lenya the ending of the story, when Jack was missing and "probably the monsters took him."

Given Lenya's imaginative, emotionally voiced reading, as her teacher, I would be sure that she had books with a range of characters with interesting relationships that could expand even further her abilities to enact intersubjective relationships and create narrative elements. Simple controlled texts won't help her develop this part of her comprehending capacities. Like Camella, Lenya's imaginative reading also might prompt me to audio-record and transcribe her stories to create a new version of *When Jack Goes Out* for her to read and revisit. This seems particularly appropriate for Lenya, who presents herself as a confident young reader eager for challenges. I might also encourage her to write her own Jack stories at the writing center. We will return to some of these ideas in Chapter 8.

Social Imagination, Narrative Imagination, and Intersubjective Enactment in James's Reading

Let's now turn to James for another example of relational aspects of comprehending. James appeared shy but confident on the day that he read *I Had Measles* with me. Once I invited him to read and he picked up the book, James was focused and attentive from start to finish. His eyes scanned the pages quickly, back and forth (left to right and right to left) as if he was apprehending multiple text meanings across pages simultaneously. He looked up and smiled at me when he was finished.

James's reading of *I Had Measles* demonstrates active and lively use of social imagination, narrative imagination, and the enactment of intersubjectivity. (For a full analysis of James's reading, see Lysaker & Arvelo Alicea, 2017.) These aspects of comprehending are most visible in his enactment and voicing of characters. The very first utterances of his reading is a character speaking in lively tones to another character: "Come awake, come awake, sister! Let's have fun. It's a beautiful day!" We can see that James quickly recontextualizes his experience of family (either his own or others he has known) and moves entirely and decidedly into the storied world. Based on his highly engaged opening utterance, we might guess that this is a hospitable text for James. His energized voicing of the younger brother character also demonstrates the emotional connection fueling this reading. James is dialogically engaged in the peopled narrative world and responding actively to the addressivity of the images.

James becomes a character himself and his voicing that character is an example of his use of social imagination. He imagines the boy on the page apparently trying to wake another character. The boy is having very specific thoughts, which he voices from the perspective of the character he has become: "Come awake, sister, come awake! Let's have fun. It's a beautiful day!" James is engaged within the landscape of consciousness via social imagination, but he is also creating new narrative elements outside this landscape when he adds that it is a beautiful day. There is nothing in the images to suggest what kind of day it is: no outside settings or window views. James uses narrative imagination to flesh out details that make sense with the characters he is enacting. He imagines that this little boy wants to go outside on a nice day to play with his sister.

James voices the thoughts, feelings, and intentions of characters throughout this reading. One consequence of James's use of social imagination to navigate the landscape of consciousness in this coauthored narrative is the construction of relationships. We already noted that in his first utterance James addresses a "sister," immediately setting up a relationship between the characters. As he moves through the story, these relationships become more complex—characters have thoughts and feelings about other characters, a kind of metasocial imagination. For example, in the first utterance of the exchange between the brother and mother on pages 4–5, James voices the thoughts of the younger brother who is thinking about the thoughts and feelings of the sick sister: "Mom, mom, she doesn't wanna come. I think there's something wrong." James's use of social imagination has led to his intersubjective enactment. His characters achieve understanding of each other. As a reader, he is dialogically enacting the realities of the people, lives, and relationships within the storied world as if he were part of it, assuming a position of sharedness and cobeing with this text.

James further demonstrates his dialogic enactment of the storied world
in the rest of this exchange. James then imagines and voices the thoughts
of the mom, who is addressing the sick sister: "Sweetie, I think you have
the measles. Let's let you sleep for a little while." He has voiced a tender moment between the mom and the sick child by using the endearment
"sweetie." This moment is made tender by his use of inflection as well. His
voice is soft and drops at the end of the utterance "Let's let you sleep for a
little while." James shifts again to the character of the little brother, who is
not so sympathetic toward his sick sister, but rather impatient and imploring for permission to play with her. "But I want her to play, mom. Can we
play? Please, please?" Again, the shift in characters, imbued with different
thoughts and emotional tones, shows James's use of social imagination that
has led him to the intersubjective enactment of the entire family in *I Had
Measles*. These activities of comprehending represent his complex, intricate
participation in this peopled narrative world as well as his deep, dialogic
sense-making.

James's deep dialogic enactment of the realities in the world of *I Had
Measles* also leads him to invent new narrative elements. His participation
in and construction of the landscape of consciousness become acts of authoring insofar as he leaves behind some of what is suggested in the images
and instead creates new narrative elements that make more sense in the
story he is authoring. He has become lead author! For example, pages 12–
13 depict the sick child looking out a window, seeing her dad and younger brother playing on the swings and the puppy running around the yard.
James ignores this outside action to focus on the thoughts, feelings, and
relationship of the father and the sick sister. This conversation becomes the
focus of James's sense-making, as can be seen in the rest of this exchange.
James voices repeated questions from the sick sister. As you can see in the
segment of his reading below, James invents a new narrative element—you
can get germs from crayons—as part of this conversation. In doing this,
James provides reasons for the dad's decision-making. James has directly
created cause and effect through narrative imagination:

> "Now can I, Dad? Can I come out of my room?"
> "No, sweetie, you can't."
> "Can I draw, Dad?"
> "No. I don't want you to get your brother sick when your, when you get
> germs on the crayons."
> "I feel better. Can we read a story now?"
> "Yes, sweetie, we can."

James also uses changes in intonation during this exchange. The dad
is somewhat authoritative and the sick child is pleading, which once again
represents James' enactment of intersubjective relationships. Characters are

imagining the thoughts and feelings of other characters and sharing in each other's realities.

James steps out of these intersubjective relationships and takes on the role of narrator in order to describe action in five of his utterances. An example of this is on page 7, when he reads, "Her dad brought her some stuffed animals and some juice." James decides that the male figure in the image is a "dad," therefore recontextualizing his own experience of male adults in families. While it may seem obvious that this male figure is likely the father, when young children read wordless books, there are no indications of characters' identities. These identities and relationships must be imagined. Many children do not give the character an identity at all, using a pronoun referent as Amber did throughout her reading of *I Had Measles* in Chapter 4.

Our noticing of James's use of social and narrative imagination as well as intersubjective enactment shows us that these relational activities make important contributions to his comprehending by (1) moving him into the vicarious social world of the story as a participant and coauthor; (2) allowing him to create and enact vibrant characters; (3) enabling him to create and enact relationships between characters in which they imagine each other's realities; (4) leading him to invent narrative elements that deepen the story he is coauthoring; and (5) enacting cause-and-effect relationships with the narrative (see Table 5.2).

Responding to James

Observing James's uses of social and narrative imagination in addition to intersubjective enactment in his reading gives us many places for conversation about his comprehending activity. My first response, an authentic and positive one, would be to tell him that I really enjoyed his reading because the characters were so lively and interesting. As a teacher, I would be interested in hearing his thinking about the process of creating them. I might say something like:

> James, what a wonderful reading you did of *I Had Measles!* The characters were so real. They were speaking to each other and telling each other what they were thinking and how they were feeling. Can you talk to me a little about how you went about making these characters from what you saw on the page? You know, James, good readers get really involved with understanding characters and what is happening between them. It helps them make sense of books they read. You are doing that here.

Depending on how the conversation went, I might next move to some specific places where James used social imagination and enacted intersubjectivity between characters.

Table 5.2. Examples of Social Imagination, Narrative Imagination, and Intersubjective Enactment in James's Reading of *I Had Measles*

Social imagination and intersubjective enactment	Imagining thoughts, feelings, intentions, and relationships	Come awake, sister! Come awake! I'd . . . ..Let's have fun. It's a beautiful day! Sweetie, I think you have the measles. Let's let you sleep for a little while. Mom, mom, she doesn't wanna come. I think there's something wrong.
Narrative imagination	Creating new narrative elements	Why can't you come outside? It's so beautiful. No. I don't want you to get your brother sick when your, when you get germs on the crayons.

James, you began your story by "being" one of the characters, the little boy who wants the sick child to wake up. You decided that the sick child was the boy's sister? Can you tell me how you chose to be that character and what it was like?

This question allows us to get a deeper sense of James's involvement in the landscape of consciousness and his use of social imagination during comprehending. This helps James see the complexity of his own comprehending and encourages him to think about his own "reading thinking," an important part of his ongoing reading development.

James, I was really fascinated by the part of your reading where you read "Mom, mom, she doesn't wanna come. I think there's something wrong." You were still "being" the little brother and you imagined that your sister didn't want to come and that something was wrong. So you were being a character imagining what another character was thinking and feeling. You really made a clear and caring relationship between the boy and his sister. Can you tell me a little about what was going through your mind as a reader? Were there parts of the pictures that led you to do that kind of imagination, or do you think it came more from your imagination all by itself?

These kinds of questions, like earlier ones, follow up on James's dialogic involvement in the storied world and help him gain insight into his own sense-making.

Lastly, I would want to talk about the two instances of narrative imagination, because they are unique contributions to the "action" of the story.

> At the very beginning of your story, James, you read, "Let's have fun. It's a beautiful day!" I know you were imagining being that little brother and wanting to have fun with your sister. How did you come to decide it was a beautiful day? I don't see anything in the illustrations that tell us that.

After letting James respond, I would point out that when readers make sense of stories, they often fill in with their imaginations in order to understand the stories as they are reading. This helps readers stay involved, comprehend, and expand what they experience as they read.

If I were James's teacher, I would do all I could to nurture his comprehending activities by making sure he had lots of complex, interesting texts to read. Given that James is beginning to read print and likely to be digesting lots of simple texts, I would offer him some more involved wordless books. *The Red Book* (2004) or *Museum Trip* (2017) by Barbara Lehman come to mind. These two books with young boys as protagonists, characters doing interesting thinking as they pursue adventures, and lots to figure out in terms of navigating and coordinating the landscapes of consciousness and action, would likely appeal to James and challenge his sense-making.

As recommended for other readers, I would also audio-record and transcribe James's reading, but for a slightly different purpose. While all young readers may benefit from seeing their wordless book readings turn into worded texts, because James is already beginning to read print, this may be particularly useful to him as a developing reader. Like other forms of language experience books, creating books with words from his wordless book narrations would result in books that are personally relevant for him to read himself. In addition, because his reading is imaginative and complex, these stories would be more interesting and complex than many of the decodable texts he may encounter.

Two cautions about responding to a reading like James's reading of *I Had Measles*. The first is not to give in to simply responding with a compliment like, "What a wonderful story!" Since James is still only in kindergarten and is demonstrating some sophisticated comprehending capacities, it could be tempting to leave well enough alone and move on to a child with greater needs. In fairness to James and to facilitating his growth as a reader, exploring his comprehending activity is worthy of time and effort. The second caution would be to resist the temptation to get James to think about whether his reading matches the images. Leading this imaginative reader to a more literal reading of this story is not likely to serve him. As suggested in Chapter 1, the question always is: What is the goal of my conversation with the child? How will what I ask lead this child forward into more complex, enjoyable, and rich participation with and within storied worlds?

WHAT SOCIAL IMAGINATION, NARRATIVE IMAGINATION, AND INTERSUBJECTIVE ENACTMENT CONTRIBUTE TO COMPREHENDING

In both Lenya's and James's readings, we can see the relational activities of social imagination, narrative imagination, and intersubjective enactment as a means by which these readers dialogically enact storied worlds and engage in comprehending. Lenya and James both use imagination to relocate themselves within the peopled narrative worlds of text as active participants. In their dialogic activity, their moving back and forth between self-experience and the meanings pointed to in the images of the book, they engage in relational activities of comprehending, imagining the realities of characters, deepening the complexity of the stories through narrative imagination, and working as coauthors. Their uses of imagination and enactment of intersubjective relationships do not result in "right answer" readings. Their narrative does not always line up with the images. They choose to leave things out. They choose to add things and go beyond the text in ways that contribute to their own involvement in the narrative world and cohere with their unfolding relationships with texts. All of this imaginative activity is what accomplished readers do while comprehending narrative texts. If we think again about Trevor in Chapter 3 or Amber in Chapter 4 who tend to stay "on the surface" describing characters and their actions, we can clearly see how social imagination and the enactment of intersubjectivity deepens readers' sense-making of storied worlds.

Lenya and James show us the power of social imagination, narrative imagination, and enacted intersubjectivity as relational activities at the core of comprehending storied worlds. Social imagination, coming on the heels of and at times merging with recontextualization, allows both Lenya and James to move into storied worlds and imagine the thoughts, feelings, and intentions of characters, as well as to create and enact their personalities and relationships. The worlds of these characters come alive precisely because of what James and Lenya do as sense-makers. From within these intersubjective worlds, James and Lenya create new narrative elements that flow from the landscapes of consciousness they have created. For both James and Lenya, narrative imagination contributes to comprehending by making people and their actions cohere across narrative time.

A careful look at James and Lenya's readings show distinct differences. Lenya, a full year younger than James and not yet in kindergarten, enacts an intersubjective world in which characters think and feel about other characters. She constructs new narrative elements that reflect these enactments. James's reading goes even deeper. His comprehending of *I Had Measles* is a good example of what Linell (2009) refers to as "full-blown" intersubjectivity. In the fullness of his enactment, his characters' personalities, relationships, thoughts, and emotions are vivid. There is intersubjective density and complexity to his comprehending. He enacts and voices several characters and relationships. He even has characters thinking about the thoughts of other characters—a metalevel of social imagination. Without hesitation, he constructs new narrative elements that give depth and coherence to his sense-making. He is intensely and dialogically engaged in the storied world and in comprehending activity.

In these past two chapters we have seen how the relational activities of response, recognition, social imagination, narrative imagination, and enacted intersubjectivity are comprehending activities that allow young readers to enter the story as participants and coauthors who navigate and orchestrate connections between the landscapes of consciousness and action. Imagination is at the heart of sense-making, expanding readers' physical realties and leading them beyond themselves into peopled narrative worlds. Imagination spurs movement from the "here and now" to the "there and then." Because of imagination, the story effectively becomes a new here and now, a place of lived experience. Both Lenya and James move through and within storied worlds as skilled sensemakers who demonstrate the relationality of comprehending. Wordless book reading gives us the opportunity to witness the imaginative relational activities of children's personal sense-making in a book context, a view of comprehending not captured by most, if any, early literacy assessment practices, and yet a critical part of reading books with words. We will continue to examine the idea of movement in the next chapter on fluency, where we see Lenya again and meet Hunter.

CHAPTER 6

Comprehending as Fluency
Prosody and Dialogic Agility

In this chapter we shift our focus to fluency and examine the imaginative work of comprehending as enacted in the movement and sound of children's wordless book readings, and the ways in which those voiced enactments contribute to their sense-making. We will observe and make note of fluency in two distinct ways. First, we will look at prosody and the prosodic use of familiar language patterns. Second, we will consider readers' movement between characters within texts, or their dialogic agility within storied worlds.

FLUENCY AS PROSODY AND MOVEMENT

It may seem odd at first to consider children's readings of wordless books from the standpoint of fluency. Generally, *fluency* refers to an aspect of print reading: the smooth, expressive, and appropriate oral rendering of an author's printed text. In wordless book reading there is neither linguistic text to be decoded nor author's language to perform with an intended phraseology. The traditional demands of fluent reading are simply not in play during children's reading of wordless books. However, while observing children's wordless book readings, it is readily apparent that the sounds of the language they use—its rhythm, pacing, intonation, and pitch—are important aspects of sense-making in this nonprint context.

While there are several definitions of fluency as they pertain to print reading (Kuhn, Schwanenflugel, & Meisinger, 2010), the most useful one for wordless book reading is fluency as prosody. In print reading, readers are expected to render someone else's text with the intonation, expression, and phrasing that represents the author's meanings. Aspects of prosody—the musicality of language—including the rise and fall of pitch, rhythm, stress, pause, and elongating sounds are all present as children read wordless books. These aspects of oral reading fluency are thought to be related to comprehension in print reading, and we will see that these same prosodic features are intimately tied to the emergent comprehending of wordless books as well.

In addition to prosody, children move through story by fluidly and flexibly representing, voicing, or commenting on different characters via social imagination. That is, young readers move through storied worlds not simply by turning pages, but by shifting positions between characters and from characters to narrator as they enact meaning across the landscapes of consciousness and action in movements of dialogic agility. We will see that this dialogic agility between characters and their relationships allows for engagement with the meanings represented by these characters in terms of both their inner worlds and their actions, and therefore contributes to comprehending. Of course, since agile movement through storied worlds is expressed through prosody, these two aspects of fluency come together in cogent, vivid wordless book reading.

LENYA AND HUNTER

In this chapter we meet Hunter and return to another of Lenya's readings. Lenya shows us how prosodic features help her move through *Float* with musicality, particularly in terms of the rhythm, pacing, and pitch of her comprehending activity. On the other hand, Hunter demonstrates the dialogic agility of moving between story characters in his reading of *I Had Measles*.

Lenya is Black and was not quite 5½ years old and midway through her pre-K year at the Head Start Preschool when she chose to read *Float* with me at the Reading Table. She settled into the reading with a quiet comfort. Hunter is White and was 6½ years old and nearing the end of his kindergarten year at one of the Early Learning Centers when he read *I Had Measles*. Hunter was all smiles during our reading session, as if reading *I Had Measles* was all he could ask for in a day. The transcripts of each of these readings can be found in the online resources for this chapter (see online Appendixes 6.A and 6.B at www.tcpress.com).

Fluency as Prosody in Lenya's Reading

All of Lenya's wordless book readings with me were full of imaginative uses of prosody to enact meaning. Most striking in Lenya's reading of *Float* is her use of the repeated phrase: "Little boy, little boy," perhaps borrowing the idea of repetitive phrases typical of classroom shared book readings. She quickly chose the book from my collection on the Reading Table and looked at the cover, authoritatively giving it a title by saying, "It's Little Boy, Little Boy Wanted a Paper Boat." Lenya uses the phrase "little boy, little boy" to begin her reading on all but three pages of *Float* (including the cover and endpapers.) While the use of a repeated phrase may not immediately seem to have to do with fluency, Lenya's use of the phrase with predictable intonation at the start of each new page enacts a rhythm and fluent musical quality to her rendering of this wordless book.

Beyond this musicality and rhythm, using the repeated phrase contributes to Lenya's comprehending in at least three important ways. First, the phrase itself points to the main character of the story, a self-initiated reminder to Lenya of the story's focus. Next, the repetition, used at the turn of the pages, helps Lenya bridge the gaps between pages as she takes in the new images that appear with each page turn. Last, the musicality and prosodic features inherent in using the predictable phrase, "little boy, little boy," makes Lenya's reading sound like story, giving it coherence and creating a particular kind of meaningful event for her. Bomer (2013) suggests that listening is an integral part of reading that allows us to hear characters and the author. In this case, Lenya is creating the sound of the story, something she will, in Bomer's (2006) words, "tune in" to during her reading. The familiar language pattern of a repeated phrase provides her with a sound context that is reminiscent of her participation in shared readings of repetitive texts in her preschool classroom.

In addition to the use of a repeated phrase, Lenya uses pitch, stress, and lengthened sounds in her expressive reading of *Float*. For example, on the title page, Lenya reads:

Little boy, little boy got some newspaper and read it the whole time. <u>But</u> he was done, he was done with the <u>new</u>spaper and he got tired.

In this example, Lenya extends the word "but," which gives it emphasis and tells us something more is coming. Phraseology leads Lenya's reading. She also stresses "news" in the word "newspaper" by raising her pitch, elongating the word slightly, and dropping her pitch at the end of the word. The effect is that we feel reading this newspaper was important but tiring, and the little boy may have wanted to be done with it. The way Lenya lowers pitch from the beginning to the end of the word "tired," confirms this bit of her sense-making, effectively expressing the boy's feeling of being tired of, and done with, the newspaper.

Lenya does something similar with stress and intonation on page 3. Here the boy is on his way out to play with the paper boat in the rain puddles. Lenya uses intonation to stress the first part of the word <u>rain</u>ing, emphasizing the boy's surprise and frustration with the rain. Lenya continues her expression of the boy's frustration in her next utterance. Her pitch rises during the phrase "on his head" and then lowers when she reads "and his hand was wet." Lenya seems to be expressing the boy's resignation to the rainstorm. Lenya also increases her pace as she reads "saw that it was raining" and "on his head," as if giving some urgency to the meaning of this phrase. Through prosody, Lenya's comprehending becomes visible in sound:

Little boy, little boy saw that it was <u>rain</u>ing. He felt a raindrop <u>on his head</u> and his hand was wet.

And the rain <u>stopped</u> when it hurt little boy, little boy's feelings.

Lenya continues using prosody to emphasize meaning on the following page. The illustration shows thick sheets of rain falling and a small figure in yellow (the boy in his raincoat) barely visible. When reading this page, Lenya uses pacing and stress patterns to show meaning. She speeds up the phrase "but it was too much rain outside," showing its importance to the story and the emotional tone of this event. She says the word "anything" more loudly than the rest, and the first part of the word <u>any</u>thing is higher in pitch than what comes before and falls into the second part of the word:

Little boy, little boy, but it was too much <u>rain</u> outside, but he couldn't see <u>any</u>thing!

These are just three examples from Lenya's reading of *Float*. Nearly all of her reading had the shape and tone of fluent, expressive reading. In these examples, fluency, particularly in terms of its prosodic features, is an important part of Lenya's enactment of meaning during her reading of *Float*. In other words, Lenya uses sound to mean. Prosody contributes to Lenya's comprehending in the following ways: (1) providing her with familiar sound contexts within which to make meaning; (2) allowing her to explore and enact variations in characters' feelings and reactions to the story events; (3) giving her a way to enact the importance of particular events; and (4) giving her the sense of being a competent reader as she hears her own story enacted in sound (see Table 6.1).

Responding to Lenya

Lenya's reading is a delightful, imaginative construction that shouldn't be harmed by too much analysis or reflective conversation. Yet, as I mentioned in my response to James's reading in Chapter 5, responding to even the most proficient readers is important to promoting their continued development. For example, there are a few things that it might be useful to investigate with Lenya in terms of fluency. After an authentic appreciative comment, I might begin by noting her use of the repeated phrase since it is a striking feature of her reading:

Lenya, you used "little boy, little boy" as part of reading almost every page in this book. I haven't really heard anyone ever do that before. Can you tell me how you came up with that idea or that phrase? I wonder why you thought you'd use it.

Table 6.1. Examples of Prosody in Lenya's Reading of *Float*

Prosody	Provide familiar sound context	Uses the language and sound of familiar books to frame her reading
	Enact importance of events	Intensity of rain:
		he couldn't see anything!
	Explore and enact variation in characters' feeling	Rain hurt little boy's feelings.

After the conversation that ensued, I would then tell Lenya that for me as a listener, her use of "little boy, little boy" made her reading sound like books I'd heard before, and made me feel like I knew what to expect.

Turning to Lenya's expressiveness, I would choose a couple of instances where the sound of her reading seemed to contribute to her comprehending:

> Lenya, you know when you were reading the pages about the little boy being in the rain, I could really tell how that little boy was feeling by the sound of your voice. On this page, when you read, "Little boy, little boy saw that it was raining. He felt a raindrop on his head and his and was wet. And the rain stopped when it hurt little boy, little boy's feelings," I could just feel what that little boy was going through. And then [turning to another page] right here at the end of this page when you said the boy's feelings were hurt I could just hear it in the sound of your voice. You know, readers who are really making sense of stories "hear" how those stories would sound. You are doing just that.

Lenya's fluent reading of *Float* tells me that she uses sound to make meaning. There are several ways to support and enhance this aspect of Lenya's comprehending. As with readers of print texts, Lenya could read wordless books to others, giving her more opportunities to develop her use of prosody in meaning-making. I would also audio-record her readings, though, unlike my earlier recommendations, not necessarily for the purpose of writing down her stories. Rather, I would offer them to Lenya for her to listen to. Having read several times with Lenya, and knowing her as a confident eager reader, I can imagine her being very interested in hearing her story as she simultaneously revisited *Float*, and even wanting to revise her original reading. I want to caution, however, that fixing up wordless book readings to somehow make them more accurate is not at all the intention. Instead, in this case, with a young child like Lenya, revisiting and hearing her own story could empower her to develop her sense-making through the use of sound.

Fluency as Dialogic Agility in Hunter's Reading

Like Lenya, Hunter was an expressive reader. His agility within the story world, rather than his prosody, contributes most particularly to his comprehending. Hunter was immediately eager, joyful, and confident when I asked him to read *I Had Measles*. (For a more thorough and developed theoretical analysis of Hunter's reading see Lysaker, 2014.) He maintained his enthusiasm throughout the reading. Hunter took great pleasure in making sense of characters and moving through the story with playful agility. My transcript of Hunter's reading, found in the online resources for this chapter (see online Appendix 6.B at www.tcpress.com), includes a marking of characters so that you can see his movement between characters during this reading. Hunter changed positions between characters 21 times in this short book and voiced five different characters: the younger sibling, sick child, mom, dad, and dog. Let's look at a couple of examples of Hunters' dialogic agility. As we know, the first double-page spread of the story shows a child in bed, apparently sick, and a smaller child and puppy, who appear to be trying to wake her. Without hesitation, Hunter reads:

> *Younger sibling:* Wake up, sister. Wake up!
> *Sick child:* Huh? What's wrong? I have the chicken hox.
> *Younger sibling:* I'll get mom.
> *Mom:* Oh, he'll be fine but it's okay.
> *Younger sibling:* But she's just like what?

During the opening seconds of his reading, Hunter enacts a spontaneous dialogue between the two children and mother, effectively voicing all three participants in the conversation with distinctive voices. His movement between characters, spurred on by social imagination, gives his reading a lively, fluid quality, and contributes substantially to his comprehending. Part of what Hunter is doing during his sense-making is listening to his own characters as he voices them. It is hearing what they say and listening to the meaning of his own utterances as they are spoken that gives forward momentum to his reading. He and the text he is creating as he narrates have become "speaking–listening" partners (Bertau, 2014; Lysaker, 2014).

Another good example of Hunter's dialogic agility is on the page 12–13 spread. The sick child is looking out the window where she sees her father pushing her younger sibling on a swing while the puppy plays in the background. Hunter reads:

> *Sick child:* Hi, Dad!
> *Dad:* Hi, sweetie!
> *Sick child:* How are you playing?
> *Dad:* I'm playing with Jeff in (inaudible).

Sick child: Why is he, why is our puppy over there?
Dad: Because, I let him go.
Sick child: Oh.

Hunter's way of making sense of this image was to enact the characters in the scene and their relationships, rather than simply describe them. By using "Dad" and "sweetie," Hunter designates identities and the relationship between the two characters. His sense-making involves not only using social imagination to imagine characters but also voicing them and moving between them to bring them to life. In his first utterance, Hunter takes the position of the sick child as she looks out the window and says, "Hi, Dad!" Then he immediately moves to the position of the father, who answers, "Hi, sweetie!" Hunter utters both these exclamations in a high pitch, representing their enthusiastic greeting. He then moves back to the sick child, who asks, "How are you playing?" The dad answers, "I'm playing with Jeff in . . . " Hunter proceeds to the child asking about the puppy (who is in the background) and finally the dad's answer. The question–answer pattern is articulated with predicable question–answer prosody; that is, the questions end in a rising intonation and the answers drop in intonation.

The dialogic agility of Hunter's reading is an important part of his comprehending. Moving from character to character demands an understanding and enactment of the characters as individual people as well as an understanding of the relationships between them. Hunter's parental characters are kind and loving; his child characters are inquisitive and interested. The relationships between parents and children are also enacted as caring, in both language and tone. Hunter's ability to enact the subjectivities of characters who know and understand each other with the affect, intonation, pacing, and rhythm of actual relationships is not only evidence of comprehending activity, but also contributes to it. He listens to the interactions he is creating, which then frame his understanding of the next moment and give his story shape. Hunter's dialogic reading builds meaning through listening and responding.

Hunter's agile shifts between different characters with different personalities allow him to traverse the landscape of consciousness and action with liveliness, speed, and dexterity. His agility contributes to a fluent reading. Speed is also worth noting here. The dialogue in the example above lasted 15 seconds in real time. While the reading doesn't sound rushed, and there are some natural pauses, there is a natural, quick pace to his reading, which, as in the oral fluency of print reading, seems to contribute to comprehending—it keeps the meaning happening.

In these few examples from Hunter's reading of *I Had Measles*, we can see prosodic enactments of dialogic agility. This expressive movement through story makes for a lively reading, but more importantly contributes to comprehending. Hunter uses movement to enact meaning. In sum,

Table 6.2. Examples of Prosody and Dialogic Agility in Hunter's Reading of *I Had Measles*

Prosody	Enacts liveliness of characters	Uses inflection to enact the personalities of the characters
Dialogic agility	Navigates broadly within the story	Voices multiple, interacting characters

dialogic agility and prosody contribute to Hunter's comprehending in the following ways: (1) They allow him to navigate broadly within the story, moving to all the characters and enacting their participation in the story; (2) they allow him to construct and enact relationships between characters; (3) the prosodic enactment of different characters gives him something to "listen to" as he enacts characters, their relationships, and story meanings; and (4) the prosodic enactment of multiple characters brings liveliness to the act of reading and brings him joy (see Table 6.2).

Responding to Hunter

Since Hunter is near the end of his kindergarten year and beginning his involvement in print reading, I might use my response to his fluency to make connections between this reading and his experiences with printed text:

> Hunter, one thing that I really noticed and enjoyed about your reading today was how you had all the characters speaking and how you moved between the characters all the time. For example, right in the beginning you created a conversation between the boy, saying "Wake up" to his sister, and the sister answering, "Huh, what's wrong, I have chicken hox." I was listening to those conversations and getting a sense of what the characters were like. I wonder if you were listening as you read? Can you describe what you were hearing when you read this page, for example?

After hearing what Hunter had to say, I might add:

> You know, when I read books with lots of characters, I imagine them speaking and it helps me really get a good picture of what is happening with those characters. I understand the book more. I think what you are doing with this reading is going to help you when you read books with words and want to make sense of characters.

As I noted above, the speed with which Hunter read *I Had Measles* seemed to contribute to his lively reading and agility between characters. At the same time, the quickness of his reading keeps Hunter from voicing characters with more depth. I might say to Hunter,

Wow! Your story of *I Had Measles* went really fast! Did you like reading that way? What do you think might happen if you read it more slowly?

Of course, as in other reading conversations, it is important to be careful not to give the message that children's wordless book readings need correction. "Reading the child" and being present to their experience of the reading will guide how you respond to individual unique readers. Given Hunter's age and energetic confidence, my sense is that Hunter would quite happily tell me what he thought about his quick reading and I would have offered an alternative for him that might be useful to his development as a reader.

To continue to investigate how quickness influences Hunter's sense-making as a reader, I would be sure to note the quickness of this wordless book reading. I would also plan to ask Hunter to read a different wordless book at my next opportunity to see if and how speed contributes to or inhibits comprehending. As we will see in Chapter 7, having children read different wordless books close together in time can help confirm or contradict our interpretations of their comprehending activity, leading to more appropriate instructional response.

WHAT FLUENCY AS PROSODY AND DIALOGIC AGILITY CONTRIBUTE TO COMPREHENDING

Considering fluency as prosody and dialogic agility points to the importance of flexibility and liveliness in young children's comprehending. Both Lenya and Hunter's wordless book readings feature qualities of fluency that seem likely to contribute to their later development as print readers. For example, the capacity for voicing characters based on sense-making is something that readers of print rely on, even during silent reading (Bomer, 2006). Emphasizing certain parts of words and sentences because they reflect one's sense-making is integral to all spoken and written language endeavors. In fact, listening is a critical part of comprehending in all interactions.

Lenya's use of the repeated phrase to invoke a "sound context" for her reading shows her ability to recontexualize genre as sound and use it to frame her comprehending of a new text. In mature print reading, the idea of sound context may be less relevant. Readers often recognize cues in texts that lead to genre recontextualizations, which can in turn support comprehending. However, such recontextualizations can afford or constrain meaning (e.g., Amber's recontextualization of the guided reading genre). On the other hand, Lenya's use of "little boy, little boy" has the feeling of playfulness, as if she is trying out a piece of language that feels good in her mouth, on her lips, and in her ears. Such play is an inquiry into language and a valuable comprehending activity for a 5-year-old.

Playfulness also comes to mind to describe Hunter's dialogic agility. He moves between characters with ease and delight, and bounces between them with the familiarity of language sounds he has likely heard in his own family. Like Lenya, the sound of his character voicings become a new resource for comprehending endearments like "sweetie," which are uttered in a kind, caring tone. Hunter's dialogic agility is in part made possible by his recontextualization of familial relationships and language use, as we saw in Chapter 4 in Camella's reading. For Hunter, this recontextualization activity is realized in the distinctive sounds of characters' voices.

Both Lenya and Hunter demonstrate that fluency as prosody and dialogic agility contribute to comprehending. For both, prosodic elements like pitch, stress, intonation, and rhythm demonstrate and contribute to their unfolding understanding of the characters they enact as they listen to the voices of those characters. Lenya's use of a repeated phrase provided a kind of prosodic support to her sense-making of *Float*. Hunter's dialogic agility, in addition to his ability to "hear" relationships develop, allowed him to voice a range of different characters, creating liveliness, and a sense of joy in his reading. While fluency is commonly assessed as a part of print reading, here we can account for fluency as it contributes to meaning-making quite directly through both prosody and agility—before words.

CHAPTER 7

Wordless Book Reading as Assessment

Over the past several chapters, we have looked closely at different aspects of children's comprehending. We began with orchestration and embodiment, moved to relational aspects including response, recognition, and recontextualization, as well as social imagination, narrative imagination, and intersubjectivity. Finally, we considered fluency. Noticing each of these kinds of comprehending activity places us in close contact with children's dialogic transaction with texts and their active pursuit of meaning with and within storied worlds. We notice the relationship between children's use of images and spoken narration and get a view of how they orchestrate meanings across visual and spoken modes. We see how children use their bodies to make meaning through pointing, sweeping, dramatization, and gaze. We pay attention to their voiced narrations, and notice the relational aspects of comprehending—response, recognition, and recontextualization—which bring children into the peopled world of story. We observe relational activity within story by noting children's use of social imagination, narrative imagination, and intersubjective enactment. Finally, close listening gives us important insight into children's comprehending activity by noting fluency with respect to their prosody, and agile movement within storied worlds.

Observing, listening, paying attention, and noting what we see is, in fact, assessment. With young children this assessing practice occurs best in what I have called "side-by-side reading." The word *assess* comes from the Old French word *assesser*, which in turn comes from the Latin, *assidere*, meaning "to sit beside." To extrapolate this meaning, "to sit beside" affords a particular kind of valuing, not possible without this very embodied positioning of "the knower." In a Bakhtinian sense, knowing and being come together (Holquist, 1990). In side-by-side reading we are present to children and copresent with them within narrative worlds. This relational engagement is compelling and intensely valuable because it allows us to know children and their sense-making deeply and intimately. This kind of knowing is the bedrock of authentic teaching (Lysaker, 2012; Lysaker & Thompson, 2013). Using wordless book reading as assessment in valid and caring ways rests on the assumption that teachers, researchers, and other participants know how "to sit beside" as relationally engaged human beings.

In this chapter we first return to some of the ideas in Chapter 1, as a brief reminder of the need for wordless book reading as an assessment of emergent comprehending. Then we will see how to make detailed observations of children's wordless book reading by using two kinds of Noticing Maps: the First Glance Noticing Map and the Digging Deeper Noticing Map. Like other informal assessments of young children's literacy, using wordless book reading with Noticing Maps can inform teachers and others about the ways in which children use particular comprehending activities as individual developing readers. As we have seen in the preceding chapters, supporting and nurturing young children's reading involves sensitive observation of their comprehending as it happens. Noticing Maps facilitate this kind of close observation and its documentation, and therefore support informed authentic teaching responses such as reading conversations, book selection, and other instructional practices meant to enhance children's comprehending activity.

WHY ASSESS EMERGENT COMPREHENDING WITH WORDLESS BOOK READING?

In Chapter 1 I suggested that understanding children's early meaning-making with books is undervalued and that assessing developing comprehending abilities prior to print reading remains a challenge both for the field of literacy in general, and for those working with young children in classrooms and other educational settings. In that discussion I also noted that assessment of subskills related to later successful print reading, such as phonological and phonemic awareness, alphabet knowledge, and phonics, persist in controlling emergent reading assessment, particularly through broadly adopted assessment systems such as PALS, DIBELS, PELI and NWEA. Even when children's comprehension is assessed it is most often through questions that require right answers to literal, text-based questions or successfully completing cloze-style retellings. These kinds of assessment tell us very little if anything about the means by which children achieve understandings, even those limited ones that might be apparent through these measures, and may also contribute to the marginalization of children whose primary form of expression is not Standard English.

In this chapter I propose an approach to wordless book reading assessment that takes into account what children do to make meaning, documenting the particular comprehending activities that are described in Chapters 2–6. It is my hope that careful observation of the comprehending activities children use during wordless book reading can provide teachers and other educators with valuable information about what children are doing as nascent readers, inform general understandings of what emergent comprehending looks like, and contribute to more inclusive and more socially just ways of assessing young children's reading. Noticing the specific aspects of comprehending as described in this book can provide a more culturally responsive and nuanced picture of what young children are doing as meaning-makers in an individually oriented book-reading context.

USING WORDLESS BOOK READING AS ASSESSMENT

Closely observing children's wordless book readings and logging the details of their comprehending activity informs our understandings of them as meaning-makers and developing readers. As in other observational assessments in the tradition of "kidwatching" (Owocki & Goodman, 2002), noticing and recording the ways in which children make meaning during wordless book reading opens doors to new ways of responding to young readers, and changes interactions between teachers and children. As mentioned in Chapter 3, being present to children as they read with the clear intent of paying attention to their unique meaning-making moments nurtures those moments as much as it informs and inspires sensitive educative response. Children thrive on reading with, to, and in the presence of interested others. Purposeful noticing is a pedagogical tool itself.

As we have seen in the preceding chapters, noticing aloud with children what they do to enact meanings with books can foster the idea that thinking about reading is something good readers do. As is true for other kinds of observational reading assessments, like miscue analysis, a retrospective conversation occurring immediately after the reading can help children see and value their own comprehending activity and build the teacher–student relationship (Lysaker, 2012). When this kind of metacognitive talk permeates caring conversations with young readers, it provides the linguistic and relational environment for learning about reading. To paraphrase Vygotsky (1978), semiotic resources first encountered in the social world become material for the personal, internal world. The availability of this material to young children is in part dependent on a trusting relationship and caring environment (Lysaker, 2012).

In order to effectively respond to what children are doing as comprehenders we need to be able to know and refer specifically to what we observe. Using a Noticing Map, like other observational assessment tools, provides a space for recording observations, for making note of what children are doing. I purposefully use the name *Noticing Map* to indicate that this kind of assessment "maps" the terrain of a child's comprehending activity and documents the topographical features of what we can see and hear. These topographical features, while not the whole story, do provide evidence of activity, which can be interpreted to make sense of children's reading. *Making note* means noticing differently; it requires purposeful focus. It changes the way we see and directs our listening, thinking, and being with the child. Of course, it also provides a permanent record of what was observed and an artifact of study for later reflection.

To illustrate how wordless book reading can be used as assessment, we will return to three of the children we have met in previous chapters and examine their readings using both kinds of Noticing Maps. First, I will describe the two kinds of Noticing Maps that can be used to map comprehending during wordless book reading and how they differ in structure and purpose from making free-form observational notes. Then I will show how both First Glance and Digging Deeper Noticing Maps can be used with Emma's reading of a single text, *Breakfast for Jack*. Next I will look at James's two readings of *I Had Measles*, which were several months apart, using only First Glance Noticing Maps. Finally, I show what happens when we use First Glance Noticing Maps to understand Molina's comprehending activity of *Float* and *Wave*, which she read on the same day.

Documenting Comprehending Activity with Noticing Maps

Before we begin working through the use of Noticing Maps with our readers, let me distinguish these maps from making observational notes. Simply observing and making observational notes of wordless book reading can be useful when children are first introduced to wordless book reading and you are interested in getting a general sense of how they are engaging in this new kind of reading. Quick free-form notes of children's level of interest, enjoyment, and stamina can be done during or after their reading. These notes can inform instruction. For example, how do children engage in reading wordless books? Is there is a need for more whole-group explorations of this special kind of text? Noting interest, enjoyment, and stamina can also help teachers make decisions about book selection. Perhaps a child does not persist in finishing the book because of its length or topic. Such information could steer recommendations for future reads.

However, in order to focus specifically on comprehending and to shape reading conversations, a more structured observation can be more useful. Noticing Maps can be used in a variety of ways depending on the purposes and the learning needs of children. To gain an initial broad and holistic view, I have created a First Glance Noticing Map, found in the online resources for this chapter (see online Appendixes 7.A and 7.B at www.tcpress.com). The First Glance Noticing Map provides a place to note what children do across all aspects of comprehending. As the name implies, the First Glance Noticing Map can be a good place to begin. First Glance Noticing Maps can be used fairly easily to assess a classroom of children at one point in time and provide a marker of individual development. The First Glance Noticing Map helps teachers document general observations about the comprehending activities discussed in this book, allowing them to see if these aspects of comprehending are present in a child's reading. For example, the First Glance Noticing Map can help them see if a child is orchestrating meanings using cross-checking, using prosody or gesture to enact meaning, or imagining the thoughts and feelings of characters.

In addition, there are Digging Deeper Noticing Maps for each specific area of comprehending also located in the online resources for this chapter (see online Appendixes 7.C– 7.F at www.tcpress.com). To explore any one aspect of comprehending (body reading, orchestration, relationality or fluency), Digging Deeper Noticing Maps can be used. As the name implies, Digging Deeper Noticing Maps allow a closer, deeper look and allow the mapping of the degree to which specific aspects of comprehending (body reading, fluency, orchestration, or relationality) are present. Digging Deeper Noticing Maps can be useful in revisiting a reading of a child that puzzles you after the reading, or to use with a subsequent reading of a child whose comprehending you are already generally familiar with from your prior use of the First Glance Noticing Map. Specific aspects of comprehending might be of interest as they help or inhibit children from accomplishing meaning-making purposes. For example, when you review the First Glance Noticing Map, if you find that you only make note of response under relational activity, you may want to look more closely at what that child is or is not enacting in terms of character meanings. As we have explored in this book, remaining in the landscape of action and staying outside of the landscape of consciousness by holding back from entering the inner worlds of characters can significantly constrain understanding storied worlds.

To prepare for a wordless book reading assessment of comprehending, you will need the appropriate Noticing Map for your purpose, a quiet space that is comfortable for the child, and the wordless book you will use. It can be advantageous to have a set of wordless books with you from which children can choose, unless you have a reason to use a specific book, something that I will address later on in this chapter. Providing children with choice can enhance their engagement with the reading, tell you something about their interests, and give insight into what they consider to be a hospitable text. It is also important to decide how much you will participate in the reading. My rule of thumb when doing this kind of side-by-side wordless book reading as assessment is to "be with" the child as an interested adult, but only actively interact in the reading when invited. This stance allows me to see what the child does independently, while at the same time remaining responsive to their meaning-making.

Video-recording of children's wordless book reading is an option that has some advantages. Using video recordings can facilitate reflection on what you observe in terms of a child's specific comprehending activities, as well as enhance your sense of that child as a reader, which in turn can assist you in addressing strengths and learning needs. Of course, video-recording of a whole classroom of children on a regular basis is often unrealistic;

limiting video-recording to children whose reading perplexes or worries you is a good place to start if you choose this option. From these video recordings you can create Digging Deeper Noticing Maps to study more closely different aspects of comprehending activity, especially for children who have already read with you. Remember that audio-recording can also be used to document fluency and relational aspects of comprehending and may be more easily managed.

Cautions About Using Noticing Maps as Assessment Tools

There are a few important points to consider when using Noticing Maps to assess children's comprehending during wordless book reading. First, like other observational assessment tools, one observation is merely a snapshot of what the child does on that particular day with that particular book. Multiple observations of children's reading are critical to being able to "see" and make sense of the complexity of a child's comprehending development. It can also be useful to observe and document children's comprehending strategies with the same book on two different occasions. Using the same book allows a view of what the reader does with particular images at different points in time and development. Observations of children reading multiple books is also informative because texts offer varied sense-making opportunities and address readers via their unique set of image-based meaning representations.

Second, as in any observation of a developmentally influenced experience like reading, the degree or intensity of a child's particular comprehending activity is not always indicative of a "better" or more sophisticated reading. As readers develop, some aspects of comprehending are internalized or abandoned in favor of new, more useful ways of sense-making. An example is children's use of their bodies. For some children, their intense use of multiple modes (gesture, prosody, and dramatization) are important to comprehending. As these same children develop, the need to externalize meanings diminishes.

Third, unlike assessments such as running records or miscue analysis, the wordless book reading assessments that I outline here are not meant to provide precise scores to be compared in discrete ways over time. Rather, the methods I explore here provide an informal, holistic sense of children's developing comprehending capacities, which can be used over time to map development, understand how children use comprehending activities differently or similarly across a variety of texts, and provide information that can guide reading conversations and instruction. Wordless book reading assessments can also be used to talk with parents about their children's reading development with the additional benefit of educating parents about emergent comprehending and the practice of side-by-side reading that they can do with their children at home.

Finally, when we observe young children's reading, we are observing the intricate and personal presence of children to texts. We are witnessing their being with themselves and others in storied worlds. These observations of children's enactment of meaning can be extremely valuable in understanding their personal sense-making and who they are as developing people in the world of books. When we use wordless book reading as assessment, we have to be careful to resist the reductive influences which permeate mainstream reading assessments and not turn something wondrous into another benchmark achievement. Doing so would negate the potential benefits of knowing children and their reading in this authentic way.

USING FIRST GLANCE AND DIGGING DEEPER NOTICING MAPS

In this section I demonstrate how to use both the First Glance Noticing Map and the Digging Deeper Noticing Maps by returning to Emma's reading of *Breakfast for Jack*. I also suggest possibilities for a reading conversation that might come from a use of these maps.

Mapping the Terrain: Using the First Glance Noticing Map with Emma

Let's begin looking at using wordless book reading as assessment by revisiting Emma and her reading of *Breakfast for Jack*. In Chapter 3 we were particularly interested in her body reading and noted that she used a range of embodied modes to enact the meanings in *Breakfast for Jack*. Remember that Emma is one of our youngest readers, just 3 years old at the time of this reading. Because this is my first experience of Emma as a reader, I will use the First Glance Noticing Map (Figure 7.1) to get a sense of how she engages in comprehending activities in general. I will use the check boxes provided to indicate which of these comprehending aspects are present.

I begin by noting the title of the book and the fact that Emma chose this book from a group of wordless books offered to her. I make a note of her general response to the book and reading event—Emma is an eager, interested reader who has confidence in her meaning-making. We know this by her initial emotional response and the fact that she chooses the book herself and initiates the reading. In fact, Emma begins so quickly that a page into the book I redirect her in order to capture the whole story. Using the First Glance Noticing Map, I also note that Emma uses her body several times during this reading. I simply check the boxes for each aspect of body reading that Emma demonstrates. Then I record my interpretations in the "Notes" section.

I then move to the "Fluency" section, making note of Emma's prosody as a narrator and her ability to move between characters from this position. In terms of "Orchestration," I indicate on the First Glance Noticing Map that Emma searches images and pauses, though only to show me something,

Figure 7.1. Emma's First Glance Noticing Map

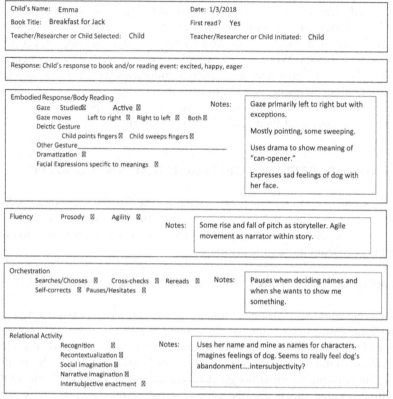

Notes: Emma is very engaged in relational aspects of the reading, both with me and with the text. She also uses her body frequently to enact and communicate meanings. Very active, lots of agency. Reading Conversation Possibilities: I'd love to explore Emma's capacity for social imagination and other relational aspects of comprehending. Revisit this book with her and find others with multiple characters.

rather than as a means of orchestrating her own sense-making. Next, in the area of relational aspects of comprehending, I record my observations that Emma recontextualizes experience to name characters, uses social imagination, and achieves a kind of intersubjectivity with the character of the dog, which she briefly voices. I make any final notes in the last Notes section and record ideas for possible reading conversations as well.

Next Steps with Emma: Digging Deeper Noticing Maps for Body Reading and Relational Activity

Given these general observations, what is it about Emma's reading that we might want to know more about? To answer this question as a teacher or researcher, I would first establish a purpose for extending the assessment.

What strikes me most emphatically about Emma's reading is her active use of body reading to enact the social and relational aspects of comprehending. As a teacher, I would want to know more about this. I may want to find other books that would nourish her burgeoning capacities for recontextualization and social imagination. As a teacher, I would also be interested in specifically noting the instances of her use of social imagination and narrative imagination, since both represent Emma's capacity for understanding nuances of character and plot, which I could nurture through reading conversations and book selection, as well as group interactive read-alouds. Because of her age and comfortable use of her body to enact meanings, I am also interested in tracing her body reading over time, particularly across different texts with different kinds of affordances for body reading. In light of these purposes, I will then choose to use the Digging Deeper Noticing Maps for the body reading and relational aspects of comprehending.

When I use the Digging Deeper Noticing Maps, I simply make check marks each time I notice a particular aspect of comprehending. For example, I mark every time Emma points to something on the page. Remember, though capturing a more detailed view of each comprehending activity is important, try to resist becoming meticulously accurate; the purpose of the Digging Deeper Noticing Map is not to generate scores, but instead to get a sense of the intensity of use. Commit to the best informal accounting of what is observed. As I review the video of Emma's reading in conjunction with the Digging Deeper Maps for Body Reading and for Relational Activity, I confirm some of my earlier hunches based on the First Glance Noticing Map and notice new aspects as well.

Let's look at her body reading first. I notice during the reading that Emma points frequently; in fact, she points over 20 times during this short reading and sweeps with her fingers four times. She points to nearly every page. This is a high-intensity meaning-making mode for Emma. In my review of her reading with video and the Digging Deeper Noticing Map for Body Reading, I also learn that her gaze is often synchronous with her hands. Her gaze for the most part moves from left to right. There are interesting exceptions, however. For example, as noted in the "Notes" section of this map, Emma sometimes looks right, then left, as she orchestrates images into a linear, time-sequenced narrative. For example, on one page there is an image of the boy feeding the cat on the right-hand side of the page, and the dog looking on a bit dismayed on the left-hand side. Emma's gaze goes immediately to the cat because it is being fed first. Her gaze is telling us that she is following the sequence of the story, rather than the sequence of the images. She constructs her narration accordingly. This, of course, is also indicative of her orchestration of words and images to form a coherent spoken narrative.

Emma also uses specific facial expressions several times over the course of the reading. These facial expressions oscillate between enacting character meanings and expressing her own response to the story. Her enactment of characters' thoughts, feelings, and intentions are quite performative, and accented when she looks at me. These facial expressions appear to have a dual purpose: to enact meanings and make sure I know what they are.

Now that I have noted instances of Emma's embodied activity on the Digging Deeper Noticing Map (Figure 7.2), I review these observations in the summary section. In line with Norris's (2004) work on modal uses, I note the intensity of each aspect of comprehending by marking a place on each line, using the intensity of the shading to indicate each activity's importance to the reading. The lighter the shading, the lesser the intensity; the darker the shading, the greater the intensity. Adapting Norris, ask yourself, "How much is the reading dependent on the use of this particular comprehending activity?" "Would this reading be the same without the use of this aspect of comprehending?" Based on my process observations and my sense of Emma's reading from sitting with her side-by-side, I determine that deictic gestures and facial expression have high intensity, while dramatization has lower intensity.

Finally, I make interpretations about the particular functions of these comprehending activities for Emma during this particular reading. For example, Emma uses her body for a range of purposes. She uses pointing to initially connect to the text as well as to lead and follow meanings across pages. She also uses her body to bring characters to life via facial expression and dramatization.

In addition to her active body reading, Emma's interest in and ability to enact thoughts and feelings of characters strikes me as unusual for her age. Very young children often stay with labeling objects and actions in their emergent reading (Elster, 1994) in part because their capacities for understanding other minds is still nascent. Because I am also interested in Emma's use of relational activity as a way of comprehending, I use the Digging Deeper Noticing Map for Relational Activity (see online Appendix 7.G for Emma's map). I make precise notes about her uses of response, recognition, social imagination, and narrative imagination. I note the intensity of each and make interpretations as I did with the Digging Deeper Noticing Map for Body Reading.

Using the Digging Deeper Map for Relational Activity helps me make sense of my first glance observations. First, by studying Emma's reading more closely, I see that she uses recontextualization and social imagination several times, and she doesn't seem to use narrative imagination. This tells me that she is able to connect and use her own experiences as comprehending tools while reading (response and recontextualization) and that she is actively using social imagination to make sense of characters' inner worlds (thoughts, feelings, and intentions). Because she does not seem to invent new narrative elements, I can also say that she "listens" closely to the text and is interested in what it is "telling" her. She also does not seem to need to invent new narrative elements to fill gaps in the text. Instead, she happily reads each set of pages as stand-alone units of meaning.

As I think through the density and complexity of her reading, I notice that while Emma often enacts single characters with intensity, she tends not to enact their relationships, with the exception of using identifiers like mom and sister. For example, she intensely enacts the feelings of the dog left behind via intonation and facial expression, but doesn't narrate the relationship between the boy and the dog: how they feel about each other, what they do together, and so on. (See Lysaker & Nie, 2017, for more on identifying relationality in young children's reading.)

Responding to Emma

I've learned a lot about Emma by using both the First Glance and Digging Deeper Noticing Maps. By noting her initial response to the reading, I know that at the age of 3, she has the capacity to be an enthusiastic, engaged reader. She is comfortable, even eager, with choosing her own books and reading with adults. Emma uses her body with joy and affect that guide her sense-making. She enacts characters in order to establish her understandings (intersubjective enactment) with me and the story characters. Further, Emma demonstrates a lively capacity for imagining the inner worlds of characters and regularly uses social imagination to enact this "landscape of consciousness," which is critical to her understanding of the narrative. However, the breadth of her navigation of this landscape is somewhat constrained. Her narration is primarily from the character of the dog. Her focus on the dog is, however, also an indication that she has keyed in on him as the main character of the story. Finally, Emma uses comprehending activity, particularly the relational and embodied aspects, for a range of purposes. In this reading, Emma shows that she can quickly and readily connect to the text using deictic gestures. She can also recontextualize personal experiences as part of her sense-making. Emma orchestrates image and spoken narration to enact meanings in a logical sequence. She moves through storied worlds, imagines, and enacts the thoughts, feelings, and intentions of characters. Finally, Emma enacts subjectivity by establishing shared meanings with people reading with her. While much of what I have recorded on the noticing maps was apparent in my simple observation of her comprehending during side-by-side reading (as discussed in Chapter 3), using Noticing Maps extends the usefulness of these observations in two ways. First, having made notations on Noticing Maps, I have a permanent record of Emma's reading and my interpretations of her comprehending activities. Second, the Digging Deeper Noticing Maps give me a more specific and nuanced view of both her body reading and her relational activity.

Figure 7.2. Emma's Digging Deeper Noticing Map for Body Reading Activity

---

Child's Name: Emma   Date: January 3
Book Title Breakfast for Jack

To use this map, note each observation of the child's specific use of body during reading with a checkmark.

In the next box, mark a place on the color gradient that represents the intensity of each aspect of body reading.

Aspects of Body Reading

Gaze
        Studied   ☒
        Searching ☒
        Rapid movement ☒
        Measured movement ☒

Deictic gesture
        Pointing ///////////////////
        Sweeping ////

Other gesture

Dramatization can opener

Specific Facial Expression //////////

Summary Intensities

Active Gaze	X
Studied Gaze	X
Pointing/Sweeping	X
Dramatization	X
Specific Facial Expression	X

In terms of responding to Emma, the Noticing Maps confirm my earlier observations and extend my interest in her relational activity. As noted earlier, I would read this book with Emma again, gently drawing her attention to the other characters—the cat and the boy, in particular—in order to lead her to a broader relational landscape. The cat is set up early in the story as a competitor for the boy's attention, and thus has a potentially strong emotional appeal. Emma indicated that she noticed this in her utterance "The cat first, the dog last," which she punctuated with a sad face. The cat,

Figure 7.2. Continued.

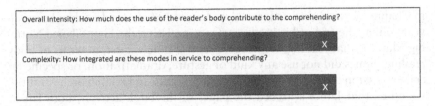

Contributions to Comprehending

☒ helps reader to enact connection to text
☒ helps reader to lead/follow meaning
☒ helps reader connect to characters
☒ helps reader bring characters to life
☒ helps reader play with word/phrase meanings

Notes

Emma's use of her body is central to her sense making. Her gaze is intense and focused and she abandons left-right convention if it doesn't support the meanings that she is interested in.

She also uses her body to enact characters and bring them to life. Though she doesn't attend to all characters. Revisit a page where she does this and ask her about it.

Reading Conversation Possibilities

Talk with her about her use of pointing, facial expression and prosody to make the story lively. Talk with her about how she uses her body to make the characters come to life. Revisit a page where she ignores a character and ask her about it.

therefore, could be a good place to start. The character of the boy is also crucial to the emotional tone of the story, which is important to Emma. Simply drawing attention to the boy could provide the impetus for Emma to attend to the inner world of the boy as she did the dog.

USING NOTICING MAPS ACROSS TIME AND TEXTS

We have seen how using Noticing Maps can help sharpen our observations of children's comprehending during the reading of one wordless book. Let's now take a look at what happens when we examine the same child reading the same book at two points in time (for a page-by-page comparison of James's two readings of *I Had Measles,* see online Appendix 7.H at www. tcpress.com).

James: One Reader, One Text, Two Points in Time

In Chapter 5, we looked at James's reading of *I Had Measles* when he was 6 years old at the end of his kindergarten year. Using the First Glance Noticing Map for that reading, we observe several things. First, in terms of body reading, James did not use any kind of gesture, dramatization, or specific facial expression to enact meaning. In terms of gaze and related orchestration, we noted that James searched the pages of the book actively, both left to right and right to left. He also paused regularly as he narrated, and "reread" or repeated lines showing that he was orchestrating his reading to allow for thinking time. Related to this, he made several self-corrections indicating that he was cross-checking his unfolding narrative with the images. He used prosody to voice different characters and to narrate like a storyteller and showed agility in his movement between characters. As discussed in Chapter 5, James's reading was intensely relational. James appears to have used recognition and recontextualization to name characters as family members. He also used social imagination frequently to enact several characters and their relationships as well as narrative imagination to create new narrative elements that reflected his enactments.

Now let's turn back the clock and look at James's reading at the beginning of kindergarten when James is barely 6 years old (see Table 7.1). Using the First Glance Noticing Map from the fall reading, we notice several things. (First Glance Noticing Maps for James can be found in the online resources for this chapter as Appendixes 7.I and 7.J at www.tcpress.com.) First, as a new kindergartner, James does not use gesture, specific facial expressions, or dramatization as comprehending activities. When we examine his gaze we can see that the movement of gaze was nearly exclusively left to right and rather calm, as compared to the very active movement of gaze from left to right and right to left seen in the later reading. One way to make sense of this is to consider that James's capacity for taking in meanings of text, to be open to responding to the complexities of its addressivity, has grown. Of course, this movement of gaze is related to the orchestration of newly perceived complex meanings into an organized meaningful spoken narration.

Further examining orchestration in this earlier reading, James pauses less, doesn't reread or repeat phrases, and never self-corrects. The less active orchestration results in a coherent but less complex and less dense narrative. Again, one way to think about this is that in the spring James is more aware of, more comfortable with, and more able to work with the complexity of text, including managing the enactment of multiple possible meanings in a coherent way. In terms of fluency, James's fall reading shows less agility as he stays in the narrator role. In relation to this role, his prosody is like that of a storyteller, without the voicing of characters.

Table 7.1. Summary of James's First Glance Noticing Maps for *I Had Measles* at Two Points in Time

Comprehending Activity	Fall	Spring
Orchestration	Some searching	Active searching
		Some pausing
	No rereading	Rereading
	No self-correction	Self-correcting
Body reading	Prosody	Prosody
	Gaze steady, left-right	Gaze active, left-right and right-left
Relational	Recognition	Recognition
	Recontextualization	Recontextualization
	Some social imagination	Frequent social imagination
	Simple relationships between characters	Rich relationships between characters
	No narrative imagination	Narrative imagination
Fluency	Prosody as narrator	Prosody as narrator and characters
	No voicing of characters	Voices characters
	Some agility as narrator	Frequent and active dialogic agility

Most striking are the differences in the relational comprehending activities in which James engages. Though he immediately recontextualizes experience by making his earlier reading of *I Had Measles* a first-person narrative—he even uses his name in the first utterance—he enacts the narrator throughout the story, staying in that position as he navigates the storied world. From this first-person position, he uses social imagination regularly, demonstrating his comprehending of characters' thoughts, feelings, and intentions, though he uses them far less than in his spring reading. In addition, and as in the spring reading, James also enacts relationships during this earlier reading, but they are less lively. James doesn't voice the characters in the fall, as he does in the spring, nor create the rich relationships that come with his "listening" and "responding" to his own narration. Finally, we don't observe James's use of narrative imagination in the fall. There are at least a couple of ways to think about this. First, as he listens to his enactment of a more complex set of characters, he is led to invent new narrative elements that come out of this complexity. For example, in the fall reading the dad is merely a character who is present and brings toys and juice (something directly represented in the images). In the spring reading, through the enactment of the relationship between the sick child and the dad, the dad becomes an authority. "Can I, Dad?" is repeated by the character of the sick child, indicating this authority. James then invents something an authoritative dad might say: "I don't want you to get your brother sick when you get germs on the crayons."

Overall, a comparison of the comprehending activities from fall to spring of *I Had Measles* shows growth in orchestration, fluency features of prosody and agility, as well as density and complexity of relational aspects. James is developing well as a reader and will soon be actively reading printed text.

Responding to James

Using Noticing Maps with James over time opens up new possibilities for talking with him about his comprehending. Since he is an older kindergartener by the time he does his second reading of *I Had Measles*, he is likely developmentally ready to think about his own reading over time. In a reading conversation with James, I might notice some of the changes apparent in the comparison of the two noticing maps with him, commenting specifically on areas of growth. I then might say something like this:

> You know James, all of these ways that you make sense of this wordless book you can use when you read books with words, too. I want you to remember what we discovered when we looked at your reading from the fall and the spring. You have a lot of abilities as a reader of stories. You use your imagination to make sense of characters and their relationships, you really search the pages to gather what you need, and then you use your experiences to understand the story. These are things that you do well and that you can also do when you are reading books with words.

I would also be careful to provide James with challenging texts for independent reading and continue to be sure that he hears complex stories in read-alouds that exceed his ability to decode as he develops as a reader of print.

Molina: One Reader, Two Texts, One Point in Time

Using Noticing Maps to observe James's two readings of *I Had Measles* provides an interesting and specific view of the changes in his comprehending activity over time. However, it can also be useful to examine children's readings of different texts at the same, or close to the same time. To provide an example of this, I will return to 4-year-old Molina, whom we met in Chapter 3.

In Chapter 3 we were specifically interested in the embodied aspects of Molina's reading of *Float*. In this chapter we will look more broadly at her reading using the First Glance Noticing Map. We will then compare it to her reading of a second book, *Wave,* that occurred immediately afterwards. Both maps can be found in the online appendixes (see online Appendixes 7.K and 7.L at www.tcpress.com).

The First Glance Noticing Maps for *Wave* and *Float* immediately reveal an abundance of body reading (see Table 7.D). As Molina reads each of these wordless books, she uses the deictic gestures of pointing and sweeping on nearly every page. Her use of sweeping is particularly notable for meaning enactment. She uses sweeping to emphasize the sadness of the boy in *Float* and the motion of the wave in *Wave*. Her gaze is on her fingers during her pointing and sweeping, indicating that she synchronously uses these modes to comprehend.

Molina also uses facial expression to show her lively response to the events in the book *Wave*. She utters an "ooh!" often as the little girl encounters the apparent ferocity of the wave. In addition, during her reading of *Wave*, Molina dramatizes and voices the little girl, loudly roaring as she imagines what the little girl is doing when she lunges at the wave with a stern face. In terms of fluency, Molina effectively uses prosody to show the emotion of characters in both texts. Her reading is modally intense; the use of her body seems integral to her reading. It is also modally complex because she uses her hands, voice, facial expressions, and dramatization to enact characters.

The First Glance Noticing Maps allow us to examine the contributions that Molina's body reading makes to her comprehending. In both readings, she uses her body to express the importance of events and characters' personalities and feelings, though she rarely creates relationships between characters. We see similarities across these readings regarding Molina's orchestration as well. She is an active reader who searches pages, scans left to right and right to left, and freely responds to images. She also pauses and repeats, particularly in her use of "then" and "because," giving her time to form her spoken narrative as she apprehends and responds to multiple images and meanings. This also affords her reading the "sound" of story.

In terms of the relational aspects of her comprehending, Molina has an open and vibrant response to both of these books. She chooses them, initiates the reading, and uses deictic gestures to enact her subjectivity in the story world. In several places, she uses social imagination to enact the thoughts and feelings of characters, demonstrating this both in language (e.g., "he's so sad") and in embodied ways (e.g., sweeping her fingers back and forth over his face to emphasize the character's sadness). We notice that she does not enact relationships between characters with the exception of simply referring to the "dad" in *Float* and by describing what the dad does with the boy: he gives him a hug and takes off his wet shirt. Molina does not seem

Table 7.2. Summary of Molina's First Glance Noticing Maps for *Float* and *Wave*

Comprehending Activity	*Float*	*Wave*
Orchestration	Searches	Searches
	Pauses	Pauses
	Repeats	Repeats
Body Reading	Points	Points
	Sweeps	Sweeps
	Facial Expression	Facial Expression
	Prosody	Prosody
Relational	Open, vibrant response	Open, vibrant response
	Social imagination	Social imagination
	Relationship implied by use of "dad"	No relationships
Fluency	Prosody	Prosody

to use narrative imagination in her reading of either book. As in James's fall reading of *I Had Measles*, Molina's enactment of characters does not demand the invention of narrative elements to maintain a coherent story. The most intense use of comprehending activity is Molina's body reading.

Responding to Molina

Looking at Molina's reading across texts on the same day helps confirm the observations of the first reading and extend our interpretations of those observations as we review them across texts using First Glance Noticing Maps. Seeing these consistencies across texts might lead to new points of interest for a reading conversation with Molina. For example, I might revisit the pages of *Float* where the boy and the dad are together, and where Molina has referred to the man as "dad," implying relationship, and say something like,

> Molina, you are so good at making me see the characters' feelings as you read, especially the boy's. Let's look at this part of the book again. I wonder what you think the boy is feeling about his dad here, or what the dad is thinking when he makes the boy some hot cocoa.

This would provide her with another opportunity to attend to and develop the boy–dad relationship.

APPLICATIONS FOR VARIOUS READERS AND LEVELS OF DEVELOPMENT

Emma, Molina, and James have given us a developmental view of comprehending activity during wordless book reading. Three-year-old Emma, 4½-year-old Molina, and 6-year-old James demonstrate that wordless book reading provides readers at different points of development with useful opportunities to engage in dialogic comprehending activities with and within texts. Are there general developmental trends that we can notice across these readers in terms of how they engage in sense-making? To answer this question, let's examine each aspect of comprehending for their different developmental trends, remembering that development is an intricate interplay of the child's unfolding bodily being with their experience (Bronfenbrenner & Morris, 2006). Of course, tracing possible patterns in comprehending across only a handful of readers has significant limitations. Still, it is a valuable way to describe and consider possible ways of accounting for changes over time.

Body Reading. Because children's uses of their bodies are most visible, changes in their patterns of body reading are perhaps the easiest to observe. As I have noted earlier, children's uses of embodied expression tends to lessen with age and experience. For example, we see Emma being very active with her body across modes and James using only gaze and prosody in his reading. Molina uses body reading fairly intensely in her comprehending, while Lenya (age 5½) primarily uses prosody and gaze like James. Molina, with less reading experience than Lenya or James, may use gesture more often to locate and guide her through the narrative landscape and sense-making. Individual differences can also create variation in when and to what degree children use their bodies to externalize subjectivities and meanings in service of their comprehending. Understanding the developmental trajectory of young children's body reading can help teachers notice unusual patterns. For example, Alice, a 5½-year-old I worked with who is not discussed elsewhere in this book, used dramatization as a primary way of sense-making during wordless book reading. Alice's spoken language was also very difficult to understand. When she read, it appeared as if she used dramatization to make her meanings clear—a wonderful and effective way to overcome her speech difficulty. In reading conversations with Alice, I would affirm her use of dramatization, but also talk with her about what happens when she reads without directly making the meanings with her body. This kind of conversation is only appropriate because Alice is at a developmental place where the modal intensity of dramatization would most likely be lessening in favor of prosody. This shift in modal intensities is not yet happening and will be required by the demands of print reading, which she will encounter very soon.

Orchestration. Searching, choosing, repeating, cross-checking, pausing, and self-correcting also seem to have a general pattern across development. Emma shows us that very young readers may be less concerned with orchestrating multiple meanings, perhaps because they are not yet apprehending those multiple meanings. Emma enacts meanings directly and confidently, without much concern for cross-checking, making self-correction unnecessary. We even see this pattern of increased orchestration with the development between James's fall and spring readings of *I Had Measles*. Noticing growth in orchestration helps teachers confirm the presence of this ability prior to children's print reading. Noticing multiple meanings with children during interactive read-alouds can support the development of their capacities for orchestration.

Fluency: Prosody and Dialogic Agility. All of the readers we have met in this book, with the exception of Amber (age 5½), use prosody to enact meaning. We saw in Chapter 4 that Amber's reading of *I Had Measles* was rather constrained. For reasons that we cannot fully know, Amber was hesitant and unsure in her rendering of *I Had Measles*. This uncertainty, as an emotional context, inhibited her sense of presence to the text. Without such presence, prosody as an enactment of subjectivity with text is not authentically possible. Prosody, then, seems less developmentally dependent and more an outcome of children's agency as meaning-makers. Dialogic agility, on the other hand, at least in terms of movement between multiple characters, seems a function both of children's presence to the text and of their openness and trust in moving within and experiencing new narrative worlds. We see agility in greater intensity in the readings of Hunter (age 6½) and James, both of whom were older, confident readers.

A sense of agency and openness to the experience of reading seems important to the development of both prosody and dialogic agility. Teachers can promote these qualities in children by creating a caring and trusting emotional tone in the classroom, particularly around reading events. Teachers can also provide a wide range of books so that children can find texts that feel hospitable. As we learned in Chapter 1, texts can make readers feel invited to participate actively in the social world of the story and respond with a sense of openness and inquiry. Active participation within story gives children a sense of the characters and their relationships, which they can then voice with prosody and move between with dialogic agility.

Relationality. Relational aspects of comprehending appear to be similarly dependent on children's capacities and willingness to be present to texts. The young readers we have met in this book have shown us different degrees and qualities of presence and the ways this presence led to relational comprehending activity. For example, in Chapter 4 Camella (age

5½) demonstrated active presence to the storied world of *I Had Measles* by frequently recontextualizing her own experiences within the story. James enacted full-blown intersubjectivity within this same storied world by imagining the thoughts and feelings of multiple characters and enacting nuanced relationships between them. Our youngest reader, Emma, actively recontextualized her immediate experiences into the world of *Breakfast for Jack* by making herself and me into characters. Throughout the story, she readily used facial expressions to enact the feelings of characters. If there is a developmental pattern here, it seems that children's initial relational response is to enact who they are and become present to text through their bodies (pointing and sweeping are common among younger children). Relational sophistication, then, extends beyond presence in the story world to the intersubjective enactment of the relational intricacies of that story world. In some ways, response and recontextualization may be earlier relational comprehending activities that lead to social and narrative imagination as well as intersubjective enactment.

Like prosody and dialogic agility, relational enactments within story are dependent on children's willingness to enter storied worlds. Caring, trusting environments can promote this willingness to engage in relational comprehending activities that, by definition, take children "away" from their actual worlds. Encouraging relational comprehending activities can also be done easily and well during interactive read-alouds during which teachers can wonder with children about the thoughts and feelings of characters, as well as their relationships and realities. As always, texts matter. Choosing appropriate texts, those that are hospitable, that have ambiguities, a wide variety of characters, and nonsimplistic emotional depictions, will help children engage in the relational activities of comprehending.

MANAGING WORDLESS BOOK READING AS ASSESSMENT

In this chapter we have used Noticing Maps to assess and value the complexities of children's comprehending activity during wordless book reading. We have used First Glance Noticing Maps to capture an overall, holistic view of this activity. The Digging Deeper Noticing Maps focus on particular areas of comprehending that are of interest. Noticing the specific aspects of comprehending gives us a nuanced picture of children's sense-making with wordless books. As teachers and researchers, these observations can tell us a lot about children as readers, inform our conversations with them, and shape how we approach instruction. Our use of Noticing Maps over time allows us to trace the intricacies of comprehending across the development of particular children as well as groups of children.

Of course, engaging in side-by-side wordless book reading, with or without Noticing Maps, and holding reading conversations takes time. In this section I would like to offer a few suggestions for managing wordless book reading as an integral part of early childhood literacy assessment.

Wordless book reading as an assessment practice could be used in several ways in early childhood classrooms. Teachers might consider adding wordless book reading to the beginning of the year assessment of literacy for all their 3- to 6-year-olds. Beyond getting a bead on the comprehending activities I have described, assessing comprehending with wordless books at the start of the year with a whole group can give a sense of the group in terms of prior experiences with reading, comfort in an adult–child reading context, enthusiasm for reading, and sense of agency as readers. This is important information and can shape instruction. For example, if most children in a class exhibit timidity or discomfort rather than enthusiasm and agency with reading, lots and lots of adult–child reading, like read-alouds and shared reads in both group and individual contexts, could be planned. While these practices are common in early childhood classrooms, I also know that they are sometimes crowded out. Wordless book reading assessment can contribute important data for why that shouldn't happen. As the school year continues, wordless book readings could be used periodically to map individual children's growth over time as differences in readings of the same wordless book can reveal interesting and important changes in children's comprehending.

While regular assessments of wordless book reading are useful in documenting growth and are recommended as informative informal sources for informing teaching, time is always a challenge. If it is not possible to use wordless book reading assessments with an entire class, choose children who stand to benefit the most. I always recommend taking that extra bit of time to try to understand the reading development of the children who most perplex or challenge you, those who keep you up at night, those who don't seem to be thriving as 3-, 4-, 5-, or 6-year-old literate beings. Yet, remember that unlike some other kinds of assessments that pull children away from instruction time, wordless book reading is an authentic literacy experience for children and is itself instructional, providing a rich reading experience for children while simultaneously giving teachers the chance to observe their reading development. This is, of course, particularly important for children whose literacy development may be of concern and who may need more, not fewer, literacy experiences.

Another consideration when choosing those children to assess using wordless book reading is the degree to which children are marginalized by assessments you are already using. As noted in Chapter 1, assessments that rely heavily on children's abilities to use, manipulate, and communicate Standard English are inevitably difficult for and biased against language differences. This group of children may include English language learners, speakers of African American English, those with speech difficulties, and even those identified with autism spectrum—an incredibly nonhomogenous group with decidedly different needs. What they have in common, however, is the need for open-ended contexts where, however language is used, it is "counted," it matters, so that honoring and nurturing personal sense-making can happen. Wordless book reading can be that context. This is not to say that wordless book reading is some kind of magical tool. I have found that some children for a variety of reasons—from comfort with English to personality, to simply not trusting yet another school task where an adult is observing closely—take a while to warm up to side-by-side wordless book reading. Hallie in Chapter 2 is an example. It was the second, not the first, wordless book reading in which she seemed comfortable, read in a voice I could hear, and seemed an active participant in meaning-making.

One side note that I think is important. Beyond benefitting children, reading conversations, in tandem with observation and documentation of children's wordless book readings, can support teachers' intellectual and personal involvement in teaching and assessment as well as their profession-al growth. When teachers become researchers and use Noticing Maps to document children's comprehending activity, they actively resist the depro-fessionalization of teachers that is robbing our classrooms and our children of intellectually and relationally engaged teachers.

CHAPTER 8

Conclusion

Wordless Book Reading in Classroom Life

In this chapter we turn to some concrete practical aspects of wordless book reading, hinted at throughout the preceding chapters, but not explicated thoroughly. We take a look at how wordless book reading can be nested into the daily school lives of young children as part of common curricular structures, as well as instruction and assessment practices. I review side-by-side wordless book reading as an everyday practice, offer more detail on holding reading conversations, suggest ways to include time for children's independent reading of wordless books, and offer ways to use wordless books with groups. In addition, I return to extensions of wordless book reading such as audio- and video-recording children's readings, as well as book making and language experience which were referred to along the way in previous chapters. I also offer suggestions for how to build a wordless book library that supports children's comprehending activities. I conclude the chapter by revisiting the value of wordless book reading for young children.

WORDLESS BOOK READING IN EVERYDAY CLASSROOM LIFE

Side-by-side wordless book reading is not the only context in which wordless books can be used to engage children in very early comprehending with books. Children can participate in wordless book reading in other ways that fit in well with the already existing early childhood literacy curriculum.

Independent Wordless Book Reading

As mentioned in Chapter 1, the children in this book attended either Early Learning Centers that housed kindergarten or a Head Start preschool. The kindergartens that Amber, Hunter, Chloe, Maya, and James attended used Reader's and Writer's Workshop as their overarching literacy curriculum. Emma, Molina, Trevor, Hallie, Camella and Lenya all attended the same Head Start program. The curricular structures used in both these settings had potential space for wordless book reading as a regular practice. Indeed, most early child curricular structures have enough flexibility to accommodate wordless book reading.

The most obvious place for the kind of wordless book reading described in this book is during independent reading time within a workshop structure. After what is usually a whole-group minilesson, children move into independent reading for an extended time. In a typical workshop approach to independent reading, children read from both self-selected and teacher-guided books on their own or in pairs as teachers hold reading conferences or small-group reading instruction (Calkins, 2001). Naturally, wordless books can be a part of what children read during this time. Independent reading of wordless books is also possible in preschool classrooms at times set aside for "choice time" or story time. In preschool classrooms, this independent time (as it often is in some kindergartens) is very social. Story-time reading is usually with friends. Thus independent reading of wordless books in preschool may be only "independent" in that a teacher is not guiding the meaning-making.

Wordless book reading can also be done in activity centers, where individuals and small groups read either independently or with adult guidance. For example, center time is a Head Start preschool classroom staple, as it is in many early childhood classrooms. Children have regular opportunities to engage in a range of learning activities with adult guidance. Wordless book reading can easily be one of those activities. A wordless book reading center, with baskets of selected wordless books and multiple copies for paired or small-group reading, can be easily created in a corner of any classroom. Including speech bubble Post-it notes for inserting dialogue with an adult's help is also an interesting addition to a wordless book reading center. The use of this material resource prompts children's relational activity with text by imagining what characters would say, inviting them into the "landscape of consciousness" and the use of social imagination.

If desired, and with adult help, digital recorders or iPads could be used to record children's wordless book reading in either audio or video files (see "Audio and Video Recordings" section later in this chapter). As mentioned in Chapter 7, wordless book reading centers can also be a place where teachers can observe children's wordless book reading using Noticing Maps to document children's comprehending activity. Using wordless book readings at centers in this way can provide another purposeful opportunity for children to engage in the independent reading of wordless books.

Side-by-Side Wordless Book Reading as Daily Practice

I have suggested in this book that side-by-side reading is a useful context for observing, supporting, and assessing young children's comprehending. It is also simply a beneficial everyday literacy practice, like reading aloud.

In fact, sitting side-by-side is perhaps the most natural context for wordless book reading with children, since it has much in common with other adult–child reading practices. Sitting side-by-side is often how we read to individual children and how we listen to children read as they begin reading books with words. However, though it is natural, I want to warn against taking for granted the importance of the side-by-side arrangement or substituting sitting across from them, which can reflect a more distant and hierarchical instructional stance.

The importance of side-by-side reading is that it is a relational configuration. We sit beside children so that the book is in front of both the child and the adult, and often both child and adult will hold the book, turn pages, and otherwise manage the material aspects of the reading. We are in a relationship of reciprocity, rather than a hierarchical one where the teacher assumes a position of authority. Instead, side-by-side reading positions the adult as someone accompanying the reader, sharing the meaning-making experience. As parents and teachers who have read to children know, sitting beside a young child reading can be filled with warmth and a sense of caring and trust.

The relational context of side-by-side reading is important because in such a context children can feel safe to take risks and be present to the storied worlds they encounter during reading. Children's sense-making requires this presence, a "here I am" that children bring to the world as a key part of their comprehending. Side-by-side reading nurtures this enactment of subjectivities and makes the outward motion of "here I am" feel safe and possible for most children. We saw Emma and Molina nearly shouting "here I am" with their bodies during wordless book reading, which was so integral to their comprehending activity. We saw Lenya and Camella recontextualize their experiences, and the language of those experiences, into their readings, extending "here I am" to "here I am in story." We saw James and Hunter further extend themselves as active agents within the relational contexts of peopled storied worlds by enacting and organizing the relationships within them through social imagination. The articulation of subjectivity is personal and makes children vulnerable; side-by-side reading sets up the possibility of a caring social environment to support this risk taking.

Side-by-side wordless book readings can happen any time during the day that children are engaged in activity and teachers are involved in observing, orchestrating, and responding to that activity, as in independent reading time in a workshop structure or "choice time" in a preschool classroom, as noted above. Such open environments provide contexts where individual side-by-side wordless book reading can happen. Side-by-side wordless book reading benefits every child and can be done informally on a regular basis, without being concerned with more focused observations using Noticing Maps. Of course, like all individual reading with children, it is time-consuming, so like other activities that require adult participation, it is best to keep records of who has had the opportunity for side-by-side wordless book reading.

Reading Conversations

As we have seen throughout these chapters, holding reading conversations with children can provide opportunities for extending and enhancing young children's comprehending. In each chapter we have seen the possibilities for responding to young readers of wordless books, focusing on particular features of their comprehending. However, while a useful part of wordless book reading assessment, reading conversations can be an authentic and natural way to respond to children's wordless book reading in a less formal everyday way, and do not always need to revolve around one aspect of comprehending. Regardless of the level of formality, reading conversations set up a time and place in which to notice and nourish each child, feed their relational capacities, and encourage their personal sense-making of text.

During reading conversations it is important to continue the tone of a trusting, caring relationship that surrounded the side-by-side reading itself, and resist the impulse to go into a more formal instructional mode. The most important aspect of the reading conversation is that the adult is really present to the child and makes the child feel that he and his reading are valuable. I realize this is not easy for busy teachers with many distractions. Also, keep in mind that very young children may not always be interested in talking about their reading. They may be more interested in simply reading more, or moving on to other things, so make reading conversations brief.

Below I suggest an outline for what reading conversations might look like. The structure and tone of these conversations are inspired by and have similarities to reading conferences for older readers suggested by Lucy Calkins (2001) and Kathy Collins (2004). You will notice that not all of the conversations I used as illustrations in this book have every element described below. Responding authentically and naturally to young readers means leaving scripted teaching behind and allowing conversations to un-fold. However, these elements are useful to consider as you think through how you want to talk with children about their wordless book readings.

- Show appreciation for the reading. "Thank you" is simple and works well, but there are other ways to show children that you feel grateful to have been able to experience their reading. "What an interesting story!" is also an open appreciative response. I have read with children where it was completely authentic for me to say, "You made my day!" having listened to their wordless book reading.
- Ask the child to show you a place in the book they really liked. This gives you a sense of what was important to the child and could also be a place where you noticed something interesting about their

meaning-making. Suggest that they share the book with a friend
if they want to talk more about it. This promotes social activity
around books that increases engagement, gives them a chance to
revisit this wordless book reading, and provides an outlet for longer
discussion.

- Continue by choosing an activity of comprehending that you
  observed that is particularly interesting or striking. Use your notes,
  noticing maps, and your experience of the child's reading to find a
  starting focus.

- Point out where you see that particular aspect of comprehending,
  returning to the book if that seems appropriate. Say aloud what
  you notice, emphasizing how you see that comprehending activity
  helping the child make sense of the story.

- Tell the child that what you have seen them do is also what
  grown-up readers do when they are reading. Using the term "good
  readers" also has its benefits since it emphasizes that you think
  the child is already a good reader. End the conversation by either
  physically giving the child a book to take with her or suggesting
  another book she might like for later reading. Having multiple
  copies of titles is helpful here, although I realize that is not always
  possible. However, physically lending the child a book at the end
  of a reading conversation can be a powerful affirmation of the
  reading and your expectations for later reading. It is also an option
  to simply tell the child about book titles that are available that she
  might find interesting.

Group Wordless Book Reading

Another way to extend individual wordless book reading is through a shared
reading approach. Much like shared reading of print texts, any wordless
book can be used in a group setting. Ms. Denny at the Head Start preschool
used wordless books with her whole group and called it "Imagination Reading." Gathering children around her in the whole-group area, she and the
class would collaboratively read a wordless book, notice detail, and negoti-
ate meanings. Often Ms. Denny would choose one child to lead Imagination
Reading, which meant that child had the privilege of holding the book with
Ms. Denny and initiating the reading. Imagination Reading was extremely
popular with the children in her class. It might seem surprising that Imagination Reading was so popular and experienced by the children as a distinct
kind of reading. There was something magical about "Imagination Reading." Without words, the power of the text was diminished and the children
gained authority as the authors of texts. This delighted them. Unlike shared
reading of predictable texts, during which children chime in on repeated

phrases and rhymes that "belong" to that particular text, during Imagination Reading the text emerged in the moment and in their words.

In addition to Imagination Reading, teachers used wordless book reading as a group experience in other ways. For example, after reading a wordless book together, children retold the story by collaboratively drawing specific story events on large chart paper. The teacher would then help the children hang these drawings in logical order on a clothesline for later re-reading. This practice is often used to retell picture books in early childhood settings. Once again, the nature of wordlessness enhanced the children's sense of agency as authors and readers, giving new importance to their retelling work. Teachers also used large speech bubble Post-it notes in whole-group wordless book reading to guide the children to imagine the thoughts, feelings, and intentions of the characters.

EXTENDING WORDLESS BOOK READING THROUGH OTHER LITERACY PRACTICES

Children's wordless book reading can be enhanced and extended by the addition of accompanying practices. Creating language experience books from audio or video recordings, encouraging children to extend their narratives in story writing at the writing center, and using listening centers as a place for children to listen to their own readings are interesting extensions of wordless book reading that can be easily added to an early childhood literacy curriculum.

Audio and Video Recordings

As noted earlier in this book, audio and video recordings of children's wordless book readings can be used in a variety of ways. Both iPads and digital recorders are useful for this purpose. Small digital recorders can be worn around the neck by teachers in side-by-side wordless book reading, while iPads are easily set on a table. iPads have the added benefit of being easily managed by young children when listening to their recordings. Young children are often interested in hearing their own voices and seeing themselves in video, and so both video and audio recordings can be well received. Letting children know why you are doing the recording gives purpose to the activity and helps them anticipate future engagement with their stories. It is also valuable to listen to children's ideas about how to use recordings of their readings, as they can imagine purposes of their own.

Creating a wordless book reading center where video-recording can be managed by a volunteer provides an easy way to integrate wordless book reading in the classroom. Making the center available on a rotating basis across a week makes it possible to gather wordless book readings from most of the class. Then teachers can view videos and decide which to map out on Noticing Maps based on the needs of the children and what becomes apparent in their readings. Also remember that older preschoolers and kindergartners can learn to record their own readings at centers with adult help.

Once recorded, children can read and reread books as well as listen to them as they would "books on tape." This practice does at least two things for young readers. First, it confirms and encourages the sense of agency readers have, since their readings are being valued through the recording process. As we saw in Chapter 4 with Camella and in Chapter 6 with Lenya, listening to their own narratives can affirm children's storytelling voice and style. These recordings can also be shared with the class as another kind of read-aloud or added to the listening center, which tells children their readings are an interesting and important contribution to the classroom community. Second, the recording allows children to revisit their stories and see how their narratives contribute to a coauthored story. While some children may want to reread and revise their readings, as mentioned earlier, the goal is never to "fix" the narratives. Rather, revisiting allows for reflection, new noticings, and another opportunity to develop their comprehending abilities.

Variations on Book Making and Language Experience

Recordings of children's wordless book readings can be transcribed and used in a variety of ways. First, for children expressing interest in print, children's readings could be transcribed onto Post-it notes and placed in the appropriate wordless books to create personalized picture books of which the children are coauthors. What once was wordless is no more! A variation of this is to transcribe wordless book readings into blank books, which children can then illustrate. This version of bookmaking is most appropriate for children who are ready for print and would be able to read some of the words they used in their wordless book narrations.

Like language experience stories, in which children use their own experiences and language to create texts, children's own narrations of wordless books make accessible and "readable" texts for children who are interested in print reading, like James in Chapter 5. In addition, using children's own words and ways of narrating creates personally relevant and more culturally aligned texts for children's sense-making with books. These hospitable texts promote the activities of comprehending as well. Books created by children using their own meaning-making represented by their own words provide a new and enticing invitation for them to reenter the storied world and revisit meanings. This is particularly important for children whose languages and narrating styles do not match the reading materials provided by their schools or push against the standardization of reading experiences;

for example, English learners or those whose speech has dialect features that differ from Standard English. As mentioned in both Chapters 1 and 7, any child whose language varies from the language used in schools can be marginalized by these differences and face difficulty in making sense of texts that don't reflect their languages and experiences.

Finally, turning picture books that have words into wordless books is an interesting variation of wordless book reading. For children intimidated by the presence of text, and therefore less likely to engage in independent reading of their favorite picture books, creating wordless book versions can be useful. To do this, cover the words of the picture book and create a photocopy version of it. Color, though expensive, is very helpful to retain the "bookness" of these reproduced versions, as is laminating the covers. In the Head Start preschool, these versions of storybooks were immensely popular, even with the older children. With the print removed, there seemed to be an enormous shift in children's expectations of what they needed to do to reread some of their favorite read-alouds. They engaged often and eagerly in reading and comprehending these wordless versions of their favorite picture books. Of course, making multiple copies can violate copyright laws, so be careful to consider these details before you proceed with this suggestion.

Building a Wordless Book Library

If you are now convinced that wordless books can make a substantial contribution to your early childhood classroom, the next challenge becomes building your own wordless book library. In the Appendix you will find a selected list of commercially available wordless books. However, I will also offer some guidance based upon the ideas about comprehending that are detailed throughout this book. As I do so, I am reminded of Rosenblatt's (1938/1983) assertion that "there is no such thing as a generic reader or a generic literary work" (p. 24). These wordless book descriptions and their potential corresponding comprehending activities are based on what I have observed in particular readings with particular children as well as what I have extrapolated from those experiences. They represent what is possible when children read these books as they transact with them. In this way, my abstraction of the books' characteristics represents my analysis of one side of the reader–text transaction. Reading wordless books with children is the only way to know how that book will function for that reader at that point in time. Keeping an open mind regarding book selection seems the best way to go. Of course, children will also point us to the most useful texts via their own book choices.

An important consideration in choosing books and in using them with children is your purpose. Wordless books used for side-by-side readings should be a manageable length for the child you are working with. I raise this particularly because many wordless books for children are quite long, and are more appropriate for individual or group exploration. For example, Ms. Savannah, a teacher at the Head Start preschool, successfully used *Journey* (Becker, 2013), meant for older readers, with her whole group of preschoolers. During their Imagination Reading, they examined each page together noticing detail, wondering about what was happening, and making comments about characters. This is valuable, but very different from, individual side-by-side reading. It is useful to have both shorter, more manageable wordless books for side-by-side reading and longer ones for personal and group exploration.

Embodiment. As discussed in Chapter 3, many young readers use their bodies to make meaning when reading wordless books. While this body reading can be done with any wordless book, or the reading of their favorite picture books, some characteristics seem particularly important to consider if you are responding to and encouraging young children's body reading. In my work with children, wordless books with some kind of dramatic action encourage children's body reading. For example, in *Wave* (Lee, 2008), the child's playful experience with a wave that becomes very large and somewhat frightening can encourage an embodied response. The implied motions of the wave, coming to and from the shore and increasing in size, inspire embodied meaning-making as readers make sense of the wave. In addition, the varied and specific actions the child takes (e.g., putting her foot in the water, reaching toward the wave, sticking out her tongue, or getting soaking wet) are all actions that children can use gesture to emphasize and dramatization to enact. *Float* (Miyares, 2015) provides similar kinds of action, as the child's boat travels down a drain and the boy chases after it, determined to get it back. Other titles that provoke embodiment are *Fossil* (Thomson, 2013) and *Chalk* (Thomson, 2010), because characters experience vividly dramatic events that invite children to use their bodies and voices.

Orchestration. Children's orchestration of meaning and transmediation of images to spoken narrative are necessary comprehending activities of all wordless book reading. However, books that suggest multiple possible meanings via ambiguous illustrations are perhaps best at prompting more complex orchestration and transmediation. For example, in *Breakfast for Jack*, Schories (2004) asks readers to navigate meanings over time on the same page. Multiple sequential images running from the top to the bottom of the page require that readers orchestrate several sets of meanings occurring over a two-page spread and make sense of multiple images that occur over narrative time within a single visual field. Another way that Schories creates ambiguity in *Breakfast for Jack* is by illustrating only the bottom half of the adult characters, as if seen from the perspective of the cat and dog. In addition to prompting the reader to navigate multiple meanings, these images provide gaps that ask the reader to imagine details that are not depicted and orchestrate them with those that are. *Jack and the Missing Piece,* also by Schories (2004), is similar in this regard. Another wordless book that prompts orchestration activity is *Sidewalk Flowers* (2015) by JonArno Lawson and Sydney Smith, which details a walk a young girl has with her father during which she picks flowers, and unbeknownst to him, gives them away. Barbara Lehman's books—including *The Red Book* (2004), *The Museum Trip* (2006/2017), and *The Secret Box* (2011)—also prompt orchestration and are even more challenging because of time sequences occurring in multiple narratives.

Fluency. Fluency in terms of prosody is necessary to all wordless book reading, storytelling, and proficient reading in general. However, prosody seems to be enhanced for some young readers with the presence of multiple interacting characters who can be "voiced" differently. This quality also contributes to inviting dialogic agility or movement between characters since there are more characters in the narrative landscape to travel between. Unfortunately, many wordless books for young children have a small number of characters. Often a single character, usually a child, encounters another character and an adventure ensues. *Float, Wave,* Mayer's *Frog* series, *Bee and Me* (Jay, 2017), *Fox's Garden* (Camcam, 2014), and *Wolf in the Snow* (Cordel, 2017) are examples of this plotline. However, the *Jack* books by Schories, because they are situated in a family context, generally have more than two characters and sometimes even characters from space, as in *Jack and the Night Visitors* (2006) and *When Jack Goes Out* (2010). *Fossil* (Thomson, 2013) and *Sidewalk Flowers* (Lawson & Smith, 2015) also feature multiple characters, although these might be considered better for older readers. *I Had Measles* (The Wright Group, 1987) is my favorite example of a book with multiple characters that can be—and in my experience often are—voiced by young readers. However, this book is currently out of print.

Relational Activities. Books with multiple characters who have relationships with one another are excellent for encouraging children's relational comprehending activities. The number and kinds of characters influence the richness and complexity of the book as a dialogic object and participation genre, which invites readers to use relational aspects of comprehending. The presence of characters having experiences—social or otherwise—gives readers experiential material to work with. Each character provides the possibility for *recognition* on the part of the reader and a relational situation that affords the *recontextualization* of experience. Readers recognize that characters living in narrative worlds "are like me," recontextualize experiences, and then narrate their thoughts and feelings based on their own relational histories. The presence of characters rendered in image also provides representations of being human that encourage *social imagination*. Each character represented in image has the potential to prompt the inter-subjective exchange between the reader and character. However, the depiction of characters in particular ways (i.e., the ambiguity of facial expression or visibility of only part of a face) seems to especially prompt readers' use of social imagination, since the characters' inner worlds are only hinted at. Similarly, vectors or invisible lines between characters, particularly as these lines represent potential eye contact with another character, signals relationship and prompts readers to imagine not only what or whom the character is looking at, but what the character is thinking or feeling as he looks. As mentioned earlier, *Breakfast for Jack* (Schories, 2004), in addition to having multiple characters (mom, dad, brother, sister, dog, and cat), uses the partial representation of characters to create a sense of ambiguity and invoke imagination—both social and narrative.

Though books with multiple characters have the greatest potential for provoking the relational activities of comprehending, even those with limited characters feature such possibility. The intensity of the main character's emotional experience seems critical to this relational invitation. In *Wave* (Lee, 2008), for example, though there is primarily a young girl and a wave (an adult woman, apparently the mother, makes a brief appearance at the beginning and end of the book), a young child's experience of the girl's wave adventure can be highly emotional. The child is at the beach alone and at the water's edge, facing the delightful yet dangerous wave. Young children respond to this with recognition, recontextualization, and social imagination. They may have had scary experiences without an adult and so imagine the thoughts and feelings of the little girl as she encounters the wave.

Other books that invite relational aspects of comprehending include Chris Raschka's *A Ball for Daisy* (2011), Matthew Cordell's *Wolf in the Snow* (2017), and Kerascoet's *I Walk with Vanessa* (2018). *A Ball for Daisy*, appropriate for our youngest readers, though only about a dog and her ball, evokes emotional response, recognition, and social imagination for children who have experienced having a dog. Daisy's conflict with another dog is reminiscent of what children go through in their own peer relationships, which prompts recognition and recontextualization. *Wolf in the Snow* also invites relational aspects of comprehending beginning with response and recognition. The story, about a young girl who gets lost in a snow storm while a wolf pup also becomes separated from its family, raises children's common emotional fears of getting lost. This recognition then invites recontextualization and social imagination.

I Walk with Vanessa, perhaps more appropriate for older preschool and kindergarten readers, tells the story of a girl who is new to school and experiences being treated meanly by a boy in her class and someone else standing up for her. The depiction of classroom and neighborhood settings with children of many shades and colors is a strength of this book and will prompt recognition for many children. The central plot line about bullying and loneliness as well as the multiple characters will invite social imagination and intersubjective enactment.

Barbara Lehman's books—*The Red Book* (2004), *Museum Trip* (2006/2017), *Rainstorm* (2007), and *The Secret Box* (2011)—in addition to prompting orchestration are also rich in opportunities for children to use social imagination. In each of these books, imagining what the characters are thinking as they live through their adventures is a central part of making sense of the book.

Of course, all wordless books draw on the full range of children's comprehending activity to some degree. This is because, as mentioned in Chapter 4, children's comprehending activities occur in synergistic ways. We distinguish them only to be able to notice and nurture them. Choosing wordless books, then, is similar, and we should be careful to appreciate them for their specific attributes, but remember that more often than not they will support children in a range of comprehending activities. Two wordless books that I think are examples of rich contexts for inviting children to engage this full range of comprehending's activities as well as attend to important current issues are *Here I Am* (2014), by Patti Kim and Sonia Sánchez, and *Bee and Me* (2017) by Alison Jay. *Here I Am* is the story of an immigrant child coming to a new place and begins with a picture of the child on a plane. The story tells how he overcomes his fears and comes to belong in his new home. It is a complex book, perhaps best used in a shared context first and with children already familiar with reading wordless books. There is the depiction of sequences of time and changes of setting that require orchestration and narrative imagination. There are multiple characters who are depicted as having complex and evolving thoughts and feelings, inviting social imagination and intersubjective enactment as well as embodied expression. *Bee and Me*, a lighter story than *Here I Am*, is nonetheless another rich context for children's comprehending. *Bee and Me* highlights the plight of honey bees in a personal story about a young girl who encounters a bee and is at first frightened but comes to care for it until it leaves. In the process, she meets another child who becomes her friend. Themes of friendship and ecology are woven together in this book. Like *Here I Am*, *Bee and Me* draws on the full range of children's comprehending activities, though at a slightly less complex level.

REVISITING THE VALUE OF WORDLESS BOOK READING

Early in Chapter 1, I posed two questions: What happens when children make meaning with books before the onset of decoding, when comprehending is the only thing that matters? And how can we think about this early comprehending in ways that break open the complex human experience that it is, lead us to value what children can do, and imagine new ways we can respond? In an effort to answer those questions, I explored a set of complicated and sometimes remarkable activities that occur as young children read wordless books and engage in personal sense-making. In each chapter I named and described some aspect of young children's comprehending, as it looks and sounds before children are concerned with words and decoding. Describing these activities answers the question of what happens, and breaks open and even disrupts what might be considered taken-for-granted ideas about what is important in emergent comprehension.

In more conventional approaches to comprehension, as I mentioned in Chapter 1, the overarching concern is children's accurate accounting of an author's text. Can the child name the characters, setting, problem, and solution for example? Can children make predictions about what will happen and check those predictions? Instead, in wordless book reading we are more interested in the *child's* text and how it is created. The special reading event of wordless book reading, particularly as it occurs in individual side-by-side contexts, captures the very enactment of the reader–text transaction. As Rosenblatt (2004) argued, when we read, we create a new text, as who we are meets and dialogically engages the meanings of the text before us, generating a set of new meanings—the unique merger of the reader and text. Almost always this new text is invisible, hidden away in our minds and hearts. But during wordless book reading, this new text becomes visible in the narratives children construct and enact with their voices and bodies. We can literally hear their meaning-making and witness their body reading giving us a view of their dialogic transaction with the text. Orchestration, body reading, response, recognition, recontextualizing, social and narrative imagination, prosody, and agility are all ways in which this dialogic transaction is enacted as the new text comes into being.

I have also shown that the aspects of comprehending these young children demonstrate in their wordless book readings are the emerging capacities necessary for deep, engaged, fulfilling, and proficient print reading. In each chapter we have noted the ways in which specific comprehending activities are similar to what children will do as mature readers. For example, as we have seen, orchestration, rather than something that is learned as a way to manage the demands of print, is used to transmediate images into spoken language during wordless book reading. In fact, orchestration is simply part of what we do in everyday meaning-making. We search, check, and adjust meanings to support our need to make meaning with others, ourselves and the world. Orchestration as an element of human sense-making is renewed and adapted for the reading of print texts where readers search, cross-check, and correct understandings as they make sense of printed words in relation to their own experience and the ongoing narrative they are reading. Similarly, the relational aspects of comprehending we have seen children use in wordless book reading—the initial response, the sense of recognition, and the recontextualization of experience that make it possible to enter narrative worlds—are critical aspects of human sense-making outside of book contexts. For example, without responding to and recognizing similarities between myself and others, empathy is not possible. Yet, of course, these relational aspects of sense-making are also required of readers of print texts as they need to imagine the inner worlds of characters through social imagination and create their own understandings of how narratives unfold using narrative imagination to invent people and events in ways that make sense in their ongoing narrative. Being agile and moving around the landscapes of action and consciousness with flexibility is similarly necessary to mature reading as well as to understanding how people's minds and actions are related in everyday life. Of course, prosody enacts meaning in our talk and storytelling as well as in the reading we do with and for ourselves and others. Enacting meanings with prosody and listening to those meanings is critical human meaning-making activity.

In this way, identifying activities of comprehending during wordless book reading prior to print reading helps us see children's comprehending as connected to and developing within their other meaning-making experiences. Of course, this has been the message of the emergent literacy perspective all along; children are becoming literate from birth (Teale & Sulzby, 1986). What I hope to have contributed to the larger project of understanding and supporting the literate development of young children is the identification of specific ways children are already engaging in comprehending activities that are contiguous with, not distinct from, what they are already doing as meaning-makers in the world and what they will do later in print reading.

I have suggested that through sensitive observation and the use of Noticing Maps, we can develop an intricate view of the *experience* of children's meaning-making, and the ways in which they participate as active agents in that experience. An account of children's sense-making experience and the comprehending activities that constitute this experience could be considered a phenomenological turn, one that highlights *being* rather than *knowing*, by noting the importance of the child's presence to, with, and within storied worlds. Beginning with the critical first move of response as the enactment of subjectivity, all subsequent comprehending activity flows from being in story. Working with and through the idea that comprehending is a way of being with and within storied worlds—a dialogic self-activity rather than a cognitive outcome—opens up new ways of understanding young children's sense-making with books. Noticing the intricacies of children's comprehending in this way values what children are doing and are able to do, while respecting the transient nature of any specific aspect of their "doingness." Children are always on their way, even as we are noticing where they are.

Of course, standards and achievement-oriented assessments of emergent reading would have us focus primarily on print-related skills like directionality, phonemic awareness, and letter–sound relationships. It is striking that in the section called "Reading Foundations" of the Common Core State Standards for Kindergarten, there is no mention of comprehension. Instead, standards considered "foundational" include "Print Concepts," "Phonological Awareness," "Phonics," and "Fluency." (In this case, fluency is concerned with children being able to keep an appropriate pace and self-correcting when reading "emergent-reader" texts.) I argued in the first chapter that this conceptualization of reading narrows literacy curricula for children and has the danger of positioning children as "less than" because development, language variation, and background make these discrete skills difficult for some children to attain within the required time frames. However, this focus also limits how teachers and other professionals think about the nature of children's meaning-making with texts.

It is also striking that in the CCSS for reading literature, every section is decidedly text-based with standards falling under the titles of "Key Ideas," "Textual Support," "Structural Elements and Organization," and "Synthesis and Connection of Ideas." Readers are nearly invisible. When readers are implied in these text-based standards, they seem to be considered unable to make meaning on their own. "With support" is the language used to describe how kindergarten children should meet standards such as "ask and answer questions about main topics and key details in a text" or "retell familiar stories, poems, and nursery rhymes, including key details." Remember that these standards are for 6-year-old children. While I have certainly suggested that relational activity during reading is paramount, the children highlighted in this book demonstrate engagement in reading wordless books on their own and enact a range of comprehending activities in the company of adults, rather than "with support." The assumption that comprehending is all about the text and is something that 6-year-olds can only do with support is problematic. In my home state of Indiana, there are also preschool standards, which are aligned with Indiana's kindergarten standards. In terms of early reading, these standards include, in the following order: "Demonstrate awareness of the alphabet," "Demonstrate phonological awareness," "Demonstrate awareness and understanding of concepts of print," and "Demonstrate comprehension." Answering questions about stories and retelling stories are listed as standards for comprehension. This view of comprehension truncates and constrains how we think about children, comprehending, reading development, and the opportunities we give children for personal sense-making with books. I worry about the ramifications of these limitations.

The purpose of this discussion is not to demonize literacy standards. Rather, I want to recognize and consider the fact that young children, even very young ones, engage in their own unique, competent, and imaginative capacities for sense-making as they read wordless books. They demonstrate rather remarkable comprehending activities, which are most often self-initiated. If I have learned anything in my years of reading wordless books with young children, it is that the activities of young children's comprehending *as it happens* constitute an important kind of lived human experience. Comprehending as lived experience is more than applying strategies. It is—if we are present to notice it—intricate, complex, human meaning-making, a way of being in the world, and, like all reading and language events, activity of self-authorship.

Comprehending depends upon the addressivity of the text and its hospitality as well as children's willingness, predilection, and capacity for response. To feel addressed by a text and to have the trust necessary to respond is critical to the kind of dialogic engagement necessary to comprehending. Children's initial response to the images of wordless books sets up an early, tenuous, and dynamic relation between reader and text, one that houses the possibility of further comprehending. If all goes well, this initial response leads to an ensuing dance of address, response, recontextualization, social and narrative imagination, and the enactment of intersubjectivities in embodied, fluent, and well-orchestrated ways. Children move around narrative landscapes with their bodies and language. They position themselves as narrators, characters, and participants in storied worlds. As we have seen, this movement involves agility and imagination within the narrative world. Living the realities of imagined others—for as briefly as a moment, for the length of the story, or the time that story continues to reverberate in the reader—engages even young children in the moral work of relating to and being with others.

When we take the time to notice the human, imaginative, and sometimes playful relational activities of wordless book reading, we get in touch with the presence of children to books as they enact their developing subjectivities in the peopled worlds of story. If we are present and pay attention, our observations of children's wordless book readings have the potential to enhance not only our knowledge and understanding of individual children and their sense-making, but of the idea of comprehending itself, and, like other ways of being with children and books, can inform and expand our view of literacy as fully human activity.

Wordless Books for Young Children

*Becker, A. (2013). *Journey*. Somerville, MA: Candlewick Press.

Becker, A. (2014). *Quest*. Somerville, MA: Candlewick Press.

Becker, A. (2016). *Return*. Somerville, MA: Candlewick Press.

*Camcam, P. (2014). *Fox's garden*. Brooklyn, NY: Enchanted Lion Books.

*Cordel, M. (2017). *Wolf in the snow*. New York, NY: Feiwel & Friends.

*dePaola, T. (1978). *Pancakes for breakfast*. New York, NY: Houghton Mifflin Harcourt.

*Jay, A. (2017). *Bee and me*. Somerville, MA: Candlewick Press.

*Kerascoët. (2018). *I walk with Vanessa*. New York, NY: Schwartz & Wade Books.

*Kim, P., & Sanchez, S. (2014). *Here I am*. North Mankato, MN: Capstone Books for Young Readers.

*Lawson, J., & Smith, S. (2015). *Sidewalk flowers*. Berkeley, CA: Groundwood Books.

*Lee, S. (2008). *Wave*. New York, NY: Chronicle Books.

*Lehman, B. (2004). *The red book*. Boston, MA: Houghton Mifflin.

*Lehman, B. (2007). *Rainstorm*. Boston, MA: Houghton Mifflin.

*Lehman, B. (2011). *The secret box*. Boston, MA: Houghton Mifflin.

*Lehman, B. (2017). *Museum trip*. Boston, MA: Houghton Mifflin Harcourt. (Original work published 2006)

Mayer, M. (1969). *Frog, where are you?* New York, NY: Dial Books for Young Readers.

Mayer, M. (1971). *A boy, a dog, a frog, and a friend*. New York, NY: Dial Books for Young Readers.

Mayer, M. (1973). *Frog on his own*. New York, NY: Dial Books for Young Readers.

Mayer, M. (1974). *Frog goes to dinner*. New York, NY: Dial Books for Young Readers.

Mayer, M. (1975). *One frog too many*. New York, NY: Dial Books for Young Readers.

*Miyares, D. (2015). *Float*. New York, NY: Simon & Schuster.

Nyeu, T. (2008). *Wonder bear*. New York, NY: Dial Books for Young Readers.

Pett, M. (2013). *The boy and the airplane*. New York, NY: Simon & Schuster.

Pett, M. (2014). *The girl and the bicycle*. New York, NY: Simon & Schuster.

Pinkney, J. (2009). *The lion and the mouse*. New York, NY: Little, Brown Books for Young Readers.

*Raschka, C. (2011). *A ball for Daisy*. New York, NY: Schwatz & Wade.

*Schories, P. (2004). *Breakfast for Jack*. Honesdale, PA: Boyds Mills Press.

---

* Books cited in the text or read by the children are preceded by an asterisk.

*Schories, P. (2004). *Jack and the missing piece.* Honesdale, PA: Boyds Mills Press.

*Schories, P. (2006). *Jack and the night visitors.* Honesdale, PA: Boyds Mills Press.

Schories, P. (2008). *Jack wants a snack.* Honesdale, PA: Boyds Mills Press.

*Schories, P. (2010). *When Jack goes out.* Honesdale, PA: Boyds Mills Press.

Stake, B. (2013). *Bluebird.* New York, NY: Schwartz & Wade Books.

*Thomson, B. (2013). *Fossil.* New York, NY: Two Lions Press.

*Thomson, B. (2010). *Chalk.* New York, NY: Two Lions Press.

Turkle, B. (1992). *Deep in the forest.* New York, NY: Puffin. (Original work published 1976)

Wiesner, D. (1988). *Free fall.* New York, NY: Morrow.

*The Wright Group. (1987). *I had measles.* San Diego, CA: The Wright Group. (Currently out of print)

References

Albers, P., & Harste, J. C. (2007). The arts, new literacies, and multimodality. *English Education, 40*(1), 6–20.

Applebee, A.N. (1978). *The child's concept of story.* Chicago, IL: The University of Chicago Press.

Arizpe, E., Colomer, T., & Martínez-Roldán, C. (2014). *Visual journeys through wordless narratives: An inquiry with immigrant children and* The Arrival. New York, NY: Bloomsbury Academic.

Aukerman, M. (2013). Rereading comprehension pedagogies: Toward a dialogic teaching ethic that honors student sensemaking. *Dialogic Pedagogy, an International Online Journal, 1.* doi: 10.5195/djp.2013.9

Bakhtin, M. M. (1981). *The dialogic imagination: Four essays.* (M. Holquist, Ed.; C. Emerson & M. Holquist, Trans.) Austin, TX: University of Texas Press.

Bakhtin, M. M. (1986). *Speech genres and other late essays.* (C. Emerson & M. Holmquist, Eds.) Austin, TX: University of Texas.

Baron-Cohen, S. (2001). Studies of theory of mind: Are intuitive physics and intuitive psychology independent? *Journal of Developmental and Learning Disorders, 5,* 47–78

Bertau, M.-C. (2007). Tania Zittoun's transitions: Encountering objects and others as a means of passage. *Culture & Psychology, 13*(3), 335–352.

Bertau, M.-C. (2014). On displacement. *Theory & Psychology, 24*(4),442–458.

Bomer, R. (2006). Reading with the mind's ear: Listening to text as a mental action. *Journal of Adult and Adolescent Literacy, 49*(6), 524–535.

Bomer, R. (2013). Common core children. In P. Shannon (Ed.), *Closer readings of the common core.* Portsmouth, NH: Heinemann.

Bronfenbrenner, U., & Morris, P. A. (2006). The bioecological model of human development. In R. M. Lerner (Ed.), *Handbook of child psychology: Vol. 1. Theoretical models of human development* (6th ed., pp. 793–828). New York, NY: Wiley.

Bruder, K. (1998). Monastic blessing: Deconstructing and reconstructing the self. *Symbolic Interaction, 21*(1), 87–118.

Bruner, J. (1986). *Actual minds, possible worlds.* Cambridge, MA: Harvard University Press.

Buber, M. (1970). *I and thou.* New York, NY: Scribner.

Bus, A. G., & Van Ijzendoorn, M. H. (1995). Mothers reading to their 3-year-olds: The role of mother–child attachment security in becoming literate. *Reading Research Quarterly, 30*(4), 998–1015.

Calkins, L. M. (1994). *The art of teaching writing.* Portsmouth, NH: Heinemann.

Calkins, L. M. (2001). *The art of teaching reading*. New York, NY: Longman.

Cambourne, B. (1995). Towards an educationally relevant theory of language lean-ing: Twenty years of inquiry. *The Reading Teacher, 49*(3), 182–190.

Clay, M. M. (1991). *Becoming literate: The construction of inner control*. Ports-mouth, NH: Heinemann.

Collins, K. (2004). *Growing readers: Units of study in the primary classroom*. Port-land, ME: Stenhouse.

Crawford, P., & Hade, D. (2000). Inside the picture, outside the frame: Semiotics and the reading of wordless picture books. *Journal of Research in Childhood Education, 15*(1), 66–80.

Dooley, C. M., & Matthews, M. W. (2009). Emergent comprehension: Understand-ing comprehension development among young literacy learners. *Journal of Ear-ly Childhood Literacy, 9*(3), 269–294.

Dudley-Marling, C. (2013). Teachers as the standard(s) bearers. In P. Shannon (Ed.), *Closer readings of the common core* (pp. 92–100). Portsmouth, NH: Heinemann.

Duke, N. K., & Carlisle, J. (2011). The development of comprehension. In M. L. Kamil, P. D. Pearson, E. B. Moje, & P. Afflerbach (Eds.), *Handbook of reading research* (Vol. 4, pp. 200–228). New York, NY: Routledge.

Duncan, R. M., & Tarulli, D. (2010). Play as the leading activity of the preschool period: Insights from Vygotsky, Leont'ev, and Bakhtin. *Early Education and Development, 14*(3), 271–292.

Dyson, A. H. (1999). Coach Bombay's kids learn to write: Children's appropria-tion of media material for school literacy. *Research in the Teaching of English, 33*(4), 367–402.

Dyson, A. H. (2015). The search for inclusion: Deficit discourse and the erasure of childhoods. *Language Arts, 92*(3), 199–207.

Elster, C. (1994). Patterns within preschoolers' emergent readings. *Reading Research Quarterly, 29*(4), 402–418.

Fuchs, T., & de Jaegher, H. (2009). Enactive intersubjectivity: Participatory sense-making and mutual incorporation. *Phenomenology and the Cognitive Sciences, 8*, 465–486.

Garte, R. (2016.) A sociocultural, activity-based account of preschooler intersubjec-tivity. *Culture & Psychology, 22*(2), 254–275.

Gee, J. P. (2001). Reading as situated language: A sociocognitive perspective. *Journal of Adolescent & Adult Literacy, 44*(8), 714–725.

Goldin-Meadow, S. (2003). *Hearing gesture: How our hands help us think*. Cam-bridge, MA: Harvard University Press.

Goodman, K. (2006). *The truth about DIBELS: What it is, what it does*. Ports-mouth, NH: Heinemann.

Goodman, Y. M., Watson, D. J., & Burke, C. (1987). *Reading miscue inventory: Alternative procedures*. Katonah, NY: Richard C. Owen.

Grumet, M. (1988). *Bitter milk: Women and teaching*. Amherst: University of Mas-sachusetts Press.

Harste, J. C., Woodward, V. A., & Burke, C. L. (1984). *Language stories & literacy lessons*. Portsmouth, NH: Heinemann.

Heidegger, M. (1953). *Being and time*. Albany: State University of New York Press.

Holquist, M. (1990). *Dialogism: Bakhtin and his world*. London, United Kingdom: Routledge.

Iser, W. (1978). *The act of reading: A theory of aesthetic response.* Baltimore, MD: Johns Hopkins University Press.

Ivey, G., & Johnston, P. H. (2013). Engagement with young adult literature: Outcomes and processes. *Reading Research Quarterly, 48*(3), 255–275.

Ivey, G., & Johnston, P. H. (2016, November). *Adolescents' diverse meaning making and the limitations of "comprehension."* Paper presented at the annual conference of the Literacy Research Association, Nashville, TN.

Jewitt, C. (2009). An introduction to multimodality. In C. Jewitt (Ed.), *The Routledge Handbook of Multimodal Analysis* (pp. 14–27). London, United Kingdom: Routledge.

Johnston, P. H. (1993). Assessment and literate "development" (assessment). *The Reading Teacher, 46*(5), 428–429.

Johnston, P. H. (2004). *Choice words: How our language affects children's learning.* Portland, ME: Stenhouse.

Kress, G. (2009). *Multimodality: A social semiotic approach to communication.* London, United Kingdom: Routledge Falmer.

Kress, G., & van Leeuwen, T. (1996). *Reading images: The grammar of visual design.* London, United Kingdom: Routledge.

Kuhn, M., Schwanenflugel, P. J., & Meisinger, E. B. (2010). Aligning theory and assessment of reading fluency: Automaticity, prosody, and definitions of fluency. *Reading Research Quarterly, 45*(2), 232–253.

Lancaster, L. (2001). Staring at the page: The functions of gaze in a young child's interpretation of symbolic forms. *Journal of Early Childhood Literacy, 1*(2), 131–52.

Leland, C. H., & Harste, J. C. (1994). Multiple ways of knowing: Curriculum in a new key. *Language Arts, 71*(5), 337–345.

Leont'ev, A. N. (1981). *Problems of the development of the mind.* Moscow, Russia: Progress.

Linell, P. (2009). *Rethinking language, mind, and world dialogically: Interactional and contextual theories of human sense-making.* Charlotte, NC: Information Age.

Lysaker, J. T. (2002). *Literacy and becoming.* Unpublished doctoral dissertation. Indiana University, Bloomington.

Lysaker, J. T. (2012). Do curriculum and instruction in schools need to be more or less programmatic? In C. J. Russo & A. G. Osborne, Jr. (Series Eds.) & A. J. Eakle (Vol. Ed.), *Curriculum and Instruction: Debating Issues in American Education* (pp. 10–17). Thousand Oaks, CA: Sage.

Lysaker, J. T. (2014). Reading as a language event of the self: In conversation with Bertua, Lipari, and Karsten. *Theory & Psychology, 24*(4), 576–591.

Lysaker, J. T., & Arvelo Alicea, Z. (2017). Theorizing fiction reading engagement during wordless book reading. *Linguistics and Education, 37*(42–51).

Lysaker, J. T., & Hopper, E. (2015). A kindergartner's emergent strategy use during wordless picture book reading. *The Reading Teacher, 68*(8), 649–657.

Lysaker, J. T,. & Miller, A. (2012). Engaging social imagination: The developmental work of wordless book reading. *Journal of Early Childhood Literacy, 13*(2), 147–174.

Lysaker, J. T., & Nie, A. Y. (2017). Social and relational aspects of comprehending in one fourth grader's unaided and illustration-aided picturebook retellings: Retelling as co-authoring. *Journal of Literacy Research, 49*(1), 38–67.

Lysaker, J. T., & Thompson, B. (2013). Teacher research as a practical tool for learning to teach. *Language Arts, 90*(3), 181–191.

Lysaker, J. T., Tonge, C., Gauson, D., & Miller, A. (2011). Reading and social imagination: What relationally oriented instruction can do for children. *Reading Psychology, 32*(6), 520–566.

Lysaker, J. T., & Wessel-Powell, C. (in press). Comprehending as imaginative, dialogic relational activity. In R. Beach & D. Bloome (Eds.), *Languaging relations in teaching literacy and the language arts*. New York, NY: Routledge.

McNeill, D. (2005). *Gesture and thought*. Chicago, IL: University of Chicago Press.

Meek, M. (1988). *On being literate*. Portsmouth, NH: Heinemann.

Norris, S. (2004). *Analyzing multimodal interaction: A methodological framework*. New York, NY: Routledge.

Owocki, G., & Goodman, Y. (2002). *Kidwatching: Documenting children's literacy development*. Portsmouth, NH: Heinemann.

Paris, A., & Paris, S. (2003). Assessing narrative comprehension in young children. *Reading Research Quarterly, 38*(1), 36–76.

Popova, Y. B. (2015). *Stories, meaning, and experience: Narrativity and enaction*. New York, NY: Routledge.

Rasinski, T., Rikli, A., & Johnston, S. (2009). Reading fluency: More than automaticity? More than a concern for the primary grades? *Literacy Research and Instruction, 48*(4), 350–361.

Ray, K. W. (2004). *About the authors: Writing workshop with our youngest writers*. Portsmouth, NH: Heinemann.

Rosenblatt, L. M. (1978). *The reader, the text, the poem*. Carbondale, IL: Southern Illinois Press.

Rosenblatt, L. M. (1983). *Literature as exploration*. New York, NY: Modern Language Association. (Original work published in 1938.)

Rosenblatt, L. M. (2004). The transactional theory of reading and writing. In R. B. Ruddell & N. J. Unrau (Eds.), *Theoretical models and processes of reading* (4th ed., pp. 1363–1398). Newark, DE: International Reading Association.

Rowe, D. W. (2015, December). *Pointing with a pen: The role of gesture in the beginnings of writing*. Paper presented at the annual meeting of the Literacy Research Association, Carlsbad, California.

Serafini, F. (2010). Reading multimodal texts: Perceptual, structural, and ideological perspectives. *Children's Literature in Education, 41*(2), 85–104.

Serafini, F. (2014). Exploring wordless picture books. *The Reading Teacher, 66*(1), 24–26.

Shagoury, R. (2008). *Raising writers: Understanding and nurturing young children's writing development*. New York, NY: Pearson.

Siegel, M. (1995). More than words: The generative power of transmediation for learning. *Canadian Journal of Education, 20*(4), 455–475.

Sipe, L. R. (1998). How picture books work: A semiotically framed theory of text–picture relationships. *Children's Literature in Education, 29*(2), 97–108.

Streeck, J., & Jordan, J. S. (2009). Projection and anticipation: The forward looking nature of embodied communication. *Discourse Processes, 46*(2–3), 93–102.

Suhor, C. (1984). Towards a semiotics-based curriculum. *Journal of Curriculum Studies, 16*(3), 247–257.

Teale, W., & Sulzby, E. (1986). *Emergent literacy: Writing and reading*. Norwood, NJ: Ablex.

Tomasello, M., Carpenter, M., & Liszkowski, U. (2007). A new look at infant pointing. *Child Development, 78*(3), 705–722.

Trevarthen, C. (2009). The intersubjective psychobiology of human meaning: Learning of culture depends on interest for co-operative practical work—and affection for the joyful art of good company. *Psychoanalytic Dialogues, 19*(5), 507–518.

Van Leeuwen, T (2005). *Introducing social semiotics*. London, United Kingdom: Routledge.

Vygotsky, L. S. (1967). Play and its role in the mental development of the child. *Soviet Psychology, 5*(3), 6–18.

Vygotsky, L. S. (1978). *Mind in Society: The development of higher psychological processes*. Cambridge, MA: Harvard University Press.

Wells, G. (1986). *The meaning makers: Children learning language and using language to learn*. Portsmouth, NH: Heinemann.

Willis, A. (2008). *Reading comprehension research and testing in the United States: Undercurrents of race, class, and power in the struggle for meaning*. New York, NY: Lawrence Erlbaum Associates.

Wohlwend, K. E. (2009). Early adopters: Playing new literacies and pretending new technologies in print-centric classrooms. *Journal of Early Childhood Literacy, 9*(2), 119–143.

Worthy, J., & Broaddus, K. (2001/2002). Fluency beyond the primary grades: From group performance to silent, independent reading. *The Reading Teacher, 55*(4), 334–343.

Zittoun, T. (2006). *Transitions: Development through symbolic resources*. Greenwich, CT: Information Age.

Zittoun, T. (2015). From Vico to the sociocultural imagination. *Culture & Psychology, 21*(2), 251–258.

Zittoun, T. (2016). Symbolic resources and sense-making in learning and instruction. *European Journal of Psychology of Education, 32*(1), 1–20.

Index

About the Author

Judith T. Lysaker is an associate professor of Literacy and Language Education at Purdue University and former first grade teacher. Her research interests include reading as dialogic, relational and imaginative activity. Specific areas of focus include reading comprehension and engagement, microanalysis of wordless book readings and picture book retellings, and teaching reading for social understanding.